NOTHING WILL BE FORGOTTEN

NOTHING

WILL BE

FORGOTTEN

FROM JAMIA TO SHAHEEN BAGH

NEHAL AHMED

LeftWord

First published in January 2022
Digital print edition, January 2022

LeftWord Books
2254/2A Shadi Khampur
New Ranjit Nagar
New Delhi 110008
INDIA

LeftWord Books and Vaam Prakashan are imprints of
Naya Rasta Publishers Pvt. Ltd.

leftword.com

ISBN   978-93-92018-24-4 (paperback)
          978-93-92018-25-1 (e-book)

Visit website

This book is dedicated to

my gurus:
Krishna Sir and Sonya Ma'am

my parents:
Saif-Matloob and Ahmedi

and my friends:
Faiza and Abhishek

Duniya ne tajarbat-o-havadis ki shakl mein
jo kuchh mujhe diya hai vo lauta raha hun main
In the form of experiences and calamities
whatever the world gave me, I am returning it

~ Sahir Ludhianvi

CONTENTS

ACKNOWLEDGEMENTS

I've never been the textbook definition of a good student; my academic life is defined by hanging around canteens chatting about all topics under the sun, distilled with a steady supply of chai. Our learning extends outside of classrooms in our canteens, gardens, and beyond. Many other students share this experience in my university, Jamia Milia Islamia; my alma-mater, Pondicherry University; and many Public Universities across India.

15 December 2019 was the darkest day of my life. On this day, the Delhi police entered our campus and beat us like animals. From that moment on, from students, we became terrorists. A few months later, North East Delhi witnessed a pogrom, and we were again branded as rioters who posed a threat to law and order.

When innocent students are labelled rioters, anti-national, and terrorists overnight, what does one do? I choose to write.

Pliant media has played a prominent role in constructing and furthering this narrative, demonizing us at every step. This distorted truth and incorrect portrayal of my identity as a Jamia student made me want to put out my version of the truth. I wrote because that seemed the only way — to document truth as I experienced it.

I wasn't sure publishing this book would be possible, and I'd like to thank many for it:

First, I want to express my gratitude to Anjana, Grace, Imran, Kopal, Kavita, Madiha, Madhuri, Navpreet, Pratimah, Vishnu, and Wasim (Bhai) for their continuous faith in me and encouragement to my writing skills.

My school teachers, Sonika Ma'am and Vandana Ma'am, and my university teachers, Adnan Farooqui, Irfanullah Farooqui,

Mohanan Pillai, Mithlesh Mukherjee, Ruchi Singh, Simi Malhotra, and Suchitra Sengupta, for whom Kabir's words ring true:

Guru Gobind dou khade, kaake lagoon paay,
balihari guru apne, Gobind diyo batay
Guru and Lord are both there, whom to adore
But teacher you are great, who told us that God is greater

I belong to stories, and stories belong to me; I collect and recollect them from people I've known, some of whom are not around today, but their stories have made me the person I am: Dada, Dadu, Badke Abba, Abbu, Mama, Afshan, Ahona, Aneesh, Anjali, Anupam, Arbina, Atif, Deepak, Divya, Huma, Iman, Imran Raza, Irfan, Jasmine, Kaifi, Kamini, Kasturi, Laimwn, Lale, Manisha, Meera, Nasima, Nimish, Phyba, Prabha, Raghvendra, Ramzan, Reyhane, Shafat, Shayan, Simeen, Ummul, Uzma, Vaani, Yasmin, Zafar, and Zainabwa.

Politics determine our past, present, and future. This book, however, comes out of my emotional vulnerability. My friends kept me going through this tumultuous time. I wasn't sure I'd be able to complete this book, but they made sure I did. Furqan arranged a place to sit and write in his hostel and fed me through the journey. Shafeeq, who read every chapter and motivated me to write on. Imran came up with a place for months, food, entertainment, peace, and so much more under the most challenging conditions. During the lockdown, I returned home, where my sister, Bella, understood my literary journey and granted me the gift of time and space.

My family is the most fun and exciting aspect of my life. Their distinct personalities and unique traits enrich my life, and they are woven into all my stories. I want to thank my brothers, sisters, nieces, and nephews. Especially my little niece, Ifrah, who I hope reads this one day.

I'd also like to thank Neyaz Farooquee, whose technical

support has guided me since the inception of this book; Arjun, Azeemah, and Shreya for giving me feedback on each chapter.

This book is a tribute to two significant women who helped me step out of my comfort zone — Rashmi Doraiswamy and Nazly Khanam.

Poets and writers who helped me understand this world and its humanity: Amrita Pritam, Amir Khusru, Anton Chekov, Bulleh Shah, Dharmveeer Bharti, Elif Shafak, Faiz Ahmed Faiz, Kabir, Khushwant Singh, Ismat Chugtai, Jaun Elia, Meer Taqi Meer, Mirza Ghalib, Neyaz Farooquee, Friedrich Nietzsche, P.N. Renu, Rahi Masoom Raza, Rumi–Shams, Saadat Hasan Manto, Sahir Ludhianvi, and many others.

Lastly, Vijay Prashad, Sudhanva Deshpande, Winnie Chauhan, and the entire LeftWord team made this book a reality. Their commitment and valuable advice transformed my manuscript into this book. They welcomed me, held my hand, guided me throughout this enriching journey — indulging all my amateur ideas and questions. I want to thank them all.

Writing this has been tougher than writing the book. If you don't find yourself here, please add your name: _____; and please accept both — my apologies and gratitude.

Thank you,
Nehal Ahmed

1. INTRODUCTION

Hum parvarish-e-lauh-o-qalam karte rahenge
jo dil pe guzarti hai raqam karte rahenge
We will continue to nourish our pen and paper
whatever befalls us, we will continue to write

~ Faiz Ahmed Faiz

On the morning of 16 December 2019, my friend Raghvendra called to ask me to visit the hospitals and police stations near Jamia Millia Islamia (JMI) university and check the status of the injured and detained university students. I rushed to the Holy Family Hospital. At the hospital gate, a journalist asked me whether I was from Jamia. I had no idea that dozens of students were lying inside the hospital's emergency ward . . . severely wounded. I wondered why was I looking for my friends in hospitals and police stations? I should be meeting them in the library, in the canteen, in the classrooms . . .

Three days before, on 13 December, Jamia students marched towards India's Parliament to protest against the Citizenship (Amendment) Act, 2019 (CAA), which activists say discriminates against Indian Muslims. It has rightly been compared with former US President Donald Trump's 'Muslim ban'. The new US President Joe Biden has since reversed that decision.

The citizenship law coupled with the proposal to implement the National Register of Citizens (NRC), aimed at identifying undocumented immigrants, spooked India's largest minority — the Muslims. They had a reason to suspect the NRC. In 2019, nearly 2 million people of Bengali origin — both Muslims and Hindus — were excluded from the NRC for Assam. Their status remains in limbo. These steps, which many Muslims fear are a part of the extreme right-wing Hindu chauvinist nationalist government's agenda to disenfranchise them, sparked India's largest peaceful protests. Instead of holding a dialogue, the government unleashed a brutal police crackdown, killing dozens of people across the country.

Jamia students wanted to march to the parliament against the citizenship law that the United Nations has dubbed — *fundamentally discriminatory*. The police dispersed the students before we could reach the Lok Sabha — the House of the People — but out of reach for us.

The next day, we went back to our classes. Everything seemed relatively unaffected. The situation, however, got out of hand very soon. On 15 December, the police entered the Jamia campus. The campus turned into a gas chamber with tear gas canisters flying around for two to three hours, sending students running to the hostels and looking for cover in the adjoining neighbourhoods.

It seems that the authorities ordered the police to storm the university campus to punish students for raising their voices. Soon the sounds of police *lathis* (batons) drowned the music of our *dafli* (tambourine) — the only weapons we had.

/ / /

On 11 December, the Indian Parliament passed the Citizenship (Amendment) Act, purportedly to provide a pathway for persecuted religious minorities from Afghanistan, Bangladesh, and Pakistan to get Indian citizenship. These three countries are Muslim majority states, which means that only non-Muslims are granted direct access to citizenship in India. For the first time, religion has overtly been used as a criterion for granting citizenship. This makes the CAA incompatible with the nation's secular fabric, a direct attack on the Indian Constitution of 1950. The attack on the Constitution attracted criticism, which translated into broad-based protests across the country, beginning from Northeast India.

Jamia played a vital role in the anti-CAA campaign that followed. On the day the CAA came to parliament, Jamia students began to protest the communal nature of the bill. Students from Jamia realized early on that it was their duty to fight against this attack on the Constitution and defend India's diversity. These protests — marches and public meetings — were peaceful and thoughtful. On 12 December, girls from Jamia organized a protest march from the Girls' Hostel to the university's main campus. Their small gathering became a considerably huge crowd; more than a thousand students joined in by the time the procession arrived at its destination. That remarkable evening shook multiple stereotypes and gave a massive push to the students to get involved in the emerging struggle.

On 13 December, the teachers' organisation called for a protest meeting inside the campus. The same day, Jamia's Students Organisation requested permission to march from Jamia to the parliament. Just outside the university, the police installed heavy barricades, blocking the road completely. We tried to break through the barricade to continue our peaceful march to parliament and demonstrate our opposition to the bill. The atmosphere was light, with slogans and revolutionary songs. The police, though, launched a lathi charge and beat the students. Our organized and peaceful protest turned into chaos — with many students beaten badly, students running here and there, and quite a few at the front of the protest being detained. This crackdown was new for us — with the lathi charge and the use of tear gas. Nobody expected such brutal action from the police. Students ran back into campus, our eyes smarting from the tear gas, hoping that we would get away, but the toxic air suffocated us even in Jamia. One student said, 'I have never seen such a scene even in Kashmir, and now I am not missing my home'. The police action exhausted the spirit of the students. We decided to sit down in protest inside our campus. The students called for a boycott of the examinations. Our administration remained silent.

The next day, on 14 December, we went to the various exam centres and appealed to the authorities to cancel the exam. We said, 'the university did not respond appropriately after such a brutal attack'. While talking to the teachers' organisation, we said that we wanted the exam to be postponed consequently. We began to protest inside Gate no. 7. The student body organized a small meeting to decide the way forward.

15 December was the first Sunday after the passage of the CAA in the Rajya Sabha. Every locality of Jamia Nagar gave a call for a march to parliament. Jamia students also decided to join the protest. Later, however, students called off this decision; it was thought that it would be better to educate and mobilize people first. On the morning of 15 December, we began a mobilization campaign in areas near the campus to inform people about the discriminatory nature of the bill. Students began to march from the campus, and residents of the area soon joined us. By the time we reached Batla House — a place in Jamia Nagar — thousands of people had joined the protest. I was at the rear of the crowd, my task to manage the traffic. After roaming through Jamia Nagar, we returned to the university. At Gate no. 7, students called off the protest. 'As students of Jamia', we said by the mic, 'we have our plan of action, and we are calling off the march right now at Gate no. 7. We are requesting all the students to get inside the campus by showing your ID cards'. The people from the locality were unhappy with our decision, and they wanted us to proceed with our protest and march to parliament. Some of the students agreed with that, and those who wanted to go went ahead. The JMI students' organisation did not give an official call for the protest to continue.

Most university students slipped inside the campus. Every volunteer was strictly advised to check university cards for those coming inside the campus; they ensured only bonafide students could do so. The majority of students went back to the campus, and I followed suit with my friends.

Due to the enormous crowd, some students did not hear that the JMI students body called off the protest. Some of these students — or those who simply wanted to — continued towards the parliament. After a little while, I saw black smoke on the side of Mathura Road. We got a call about a brutal police lathi charge and the firing of tear gas at the march in no time. The police chased after the protestors. We watched from inside the campus, which is not a closed-door campus.

The military atmosphere near the campus scared the students. I was sure that the police would fire tear gas inside the campus, even if they would not enter the premises. Many other students agreed with me because most of the protestors were outside the campus; what was the need for the police to enter the campus? *However, the police did break through the Library Gate, did enter the campus, did fire tear gas into the campus, and did beat the students mercilessly, damaging university property.*

The police first cornered us with tear gas, then hit students in every corner of the campus, and finally tried to evacuate the students from campus. Videos of the brutality inside the library, in particular, spread around the world. We managed to save ourselves and take refuge from the police violence. There was some relief for students, which was the solidarity we received from JMI alumni and others around the world; this response gave us hope and powered our fight against this brutal attack. The residents of Jamia Nagar blocked the highway in Shaheen Bagh, which connects Delhi and Noida. They began a sit-in protest on the road, which became the epicentre of the national campaign against CAA-NRC.

The next day, 16 December, we searched for our friends in hospitals and police stations. Our full-scale protest started then. On 17 December, Jamia students formed the Jamia Coordination

Committee (JCC) — which gathered the student organisations, the Jamia teachers and the Jamia alumni. The committee consisted of 50 members. They created a WhatsApp group and several sub-committees for media, medical care, logistics, and so on.

/   /   /

History repeats itself! JMI was a crucial part of Gandhi's 1920 Non-Cooperation Movement, only a year old back then. In 2019, Jamia — at hundred years old — recovered that tradition and stood for the nationalist values that created our university. We pledged to defend and deepen the idea of India.

2. PALESTINE AND JAMIA

Ae arz-e-Falasteen! Main bhi hazir hun
Oh, the earth of Palestine: I too am yours

~ Habib Jalib

In October 2019, the Faculty of Architecture and Ekistics organized the Global Health Zenith Confluence, with Israel as the country partner. The presence of Israel anguished the students. About twenty students began a symbolic protest around Israel's participation. The university officials approached this protest not as an opportunity for dialogue but as a law-and-order problem. Security guards were called in, and two students were picked up, beaten, and then locked in the proctor's office. The proctor informed other students about the arrest. Some students requested the students' release, but the administration would not even entertain their entreaty. The administration issued a show-cause notice to five students for protesting Israel's participation.

I was in Class 6 when the Palestinian leader, Yasser Arafat, passed away in 2004. It was then that the idea of Palestine came alive to me and many of my generation. Eight years later, in November 2012, Israel pummelled the Gaza Strip with dangerous munitions for eight days, killing more than 150 people and injuring more than a thousand Palestinians. The enormity of Israel's assault impacted the Jamia community. The Outreach Programme and Indo-Arab Cultural Centre of JMI organized a protest march in solidarity with Palestine on 23 November 2012. Teachers, students, and university staff marched along with vice-chancellor Najeeb Jung and the Palestinian Ambassador to India, Adil Shaban Hassan Sadiq. I was then an undergraduate, profoundly impacted by that week of bombing and the march itself. I learned what it

21

meant to be a concerned student — concerned for humanity and for the ethos of my nation. Our solidarity with Palestine was not limited to the fact that most Palestinians are Muslims; we stood with Palestine because we believe in decolonization and building a world without discrimination of any kind.

Jamia is not merely a university, it is a child of the Indian Independence Movement. Among Jamia's many well-known founders was a lesser-known personality — Gerda Philipsborn. Hers is the heart-warming story of a German Jew, fondly addressed as *appa jan* (dear elder sister), who fled from her country to ours just before the Nazis came to power.

Gerda joined Jamia on 1 January 1933 and served till she breathed her last on 14 April 1943. She was in charge of the daycare centre of Jamia and helped in many sections of the university. She travelled across the country to raise funds for the Jamia, started the university magazine and organised a women's seminar. Also known as *Khatoon-e-Awwal* — Jamia's Woman Number One — for her immense contributions and dedication.

The founders of Jamia formed personal and institutional relationships with the German intelligentsia, which was dominated by Jews. It offered space to a German Jew woman who was forced to leave her country because of fascism. The same Jamia stands against the 'Jewish' nation Israel. In both cases, religion does not matter. Jamia stood for humanity and against oppression — Nazi oppression then and Zionist oppression now.

India's commitment to Palestine withered in 1992 when India normalized relations with Israel. In 2003, Israel's Prime Minister Ariel Sharon visited India, and then in 2018, India's Prime Minister Narendra Modi visited Israel — both firsts. In this context of normalization, Jamia hosted an event with Israel as the country partner; but it was in the context of India's long tradition of support for Palestine that the students took action.

Due to the show-cause notice against the students on the Palestine issue, others started a 24-hour sit-in on 14 October 2019.

These sit-in protests were novel for Jamia, where the administration had tried to narrow the political space. During my orientation programme for the undergraduate degree in 2012, vice-chancellor Najeeb Jung said, 'The university is not a political ground where you should train to become MLAs and MPs. It would be best to prepare for the IAS and the IPS'. He did not allow students to put up political posters on the walls. It was during his tenure that security guards began to suffocate dissent. They often employed retired army officers, and their attitude toward checking our IDs made us feel like we lived on India's borders. I completed my BA in Political Science in 2015, having studied during the tenure of vice-chancellor Najeeb Jung. I still feel miserable about that, about the fact that I studied when the vice-chancellor had banned political activity on the campus and operated in a dictatorial fashion.

Because of the attack on dissent on Jamia's campus, only a few students and their organisations joined the 14 October 2019 sit-in. On the ninth day of the protest, on 23 October, the students called for a march to the vice-chancellor's office. About a hundred students began the march, which eventually swelled into a vast crowd. I also joined the protest.

We drew up a precise list of demands:

1. Withdraw the show cause notice against the students.
2. No action should be taken against the students.
3. The chief proctor must issue a letter of apology to the students.
4. Disciplinary action must be taken against the guards.
5. Action must be taken against the proctor's staff for manhandling the students.

We stood in front of the vice-chancellor's office with our simple demands. Nobody came to listen to our grievances. A couple of times, the officials came to warn us or suggest some impractical solutions to our demands. That afternoon, we felt that the movement had impacted the campus; just by being here, by breaking the grip of what Najeeb Jung had done to campus politics, we had succeeded.

Around 6 pm that day, a few goons entered from the main gate of the vice-chancellor's office; this gate was supposed to be guarded by security — mainly retired army men — and the police. These goons came directly toward those of us who were sitting in protest at the VC office gate. We did not realize what was happening until they began to beat us and molest female students, breaking the flowerpots and the decorative lights in their rage. We managed to run away (although many students suffered injuries and one even required hospitalization). No guards came to save the students, nor had they stopped the goons from entering the campus; it was clear that there was collusion between the security guards and the goons. The appearance of the goons — some students, some non-students — has become familiar on campus. Some months earlier, at a protest over allegations of sexual misconduct by the head of the Applied Arts department, goons attacked the protestors; even in that instance, the administration did not take any action against the goons or the accused department head.

On the evening of 23 October, stunningly, the university's media coordinator stated that the violence stemmed from a fight between a student of the English Department and a protestor. Coinciding with the protest, the English Department held a seminar in a building just behind the VC's office. Many students from the English department joined the protest. There was no fight amongst the students. Why did the university administration release a false statement to the media? CCTV cameras cover the entire area, so the authorities had the option to study them and hand the culprits over to the police. If it were true that the students from the English department were involved, then why did the university not act against them?

Till this attack, Jamia had been a very apolitical campus, driven partially by the policies of the vice-chancellor Najeeb Jung.

Students were happy to limit themselves to studies (class, seminar, and the library) and social life (the canteen and the hostels). Few students on campus seemed to be politically aware, and if they were, they associated themselves with political parties and did their work elsewhere. That evening, something unusual happened at Jamia. News of the attack spread across the campus and Delhi. The media came to cover the story. That was when students left their *padhai-likhai* (academic work) and revived the older traditions of struggle by Jamia students. Around 8 pm, students began to arrive at the protest site, boosting the morale of the students who had been at the sit-down strike for the past nine days.

On that evening — 23 October, the ninth day of the protest — students blocked the road towards the vice-chancellor's office. The students called for a complete lockdown of campus on 24 October. Students from all departments supported the call. The following day, Jamia students walked with the air of revolutionaries. We captured the entire campus: classes boycotted, roads blocked. We gathered in front of the vice-chancellor's office, joining the students who had been there since 14 October. This site became the centre of Jamia, with several activities taking place there to revive the democratic culture of the university. Everything seemed novel to the students.

By the afternoon, the administration asked some students to come to the proctor's office to present their demands. The negotiation went on for the rest of the day. The fight was not for something directly related to Jamia only, but it linked Jamia's concerns to the world, in this case, to Palestine.

At 8 pm, a female student activist emerged from the proctor's office with a piece of paper. She stood at the centre of the protest site and raised slogans against the Jamia administration's positive attitude toward Israel. I was standing in a corner and watched the student — who I did not recognize — reading out our demands, which the Jamia administration accepted. We had raised our voices for the freedom of Palestine. It was exhilarating.

We decided to conduct a victory march. We marched to the central library, which is on the main campus, inside Gate no. 7. On the stairs to the central library, the students gathered and raised slogans — our voices filled with happiness — which united students from various political parties and commitments in this struggle. It was a historic moment for Jamia.

By 9 pm, thousands of students gathered in front of the library, where lights were bright and suggested the graceful mood of the students. We began by condemning an association of the campus with Israel — a power that is occupying the Palestinian people — and we ended by deepening the democratic spirit inside Jamia. The havoc created by the vice-chancellors — Najeeb Jung and Talat Ahmed — was now settled on the students' side, the administration's anti-democratic attitude set aside.

/ / /

On the evening of 24 October, my batchmates began to call and congratulate the students. They were surprised. Everyone was surprised to see such a revolutionary act at Jamia.

I graduated with a BA degree from Jamia in 2015. I was a dedicated student activist and a cardholder member of a student organisation during my undergraduate years. I was always prepared to raise my voice against any form of injustice, whether inside or outside of India. We issued condemnation letters and wrote our views on the campus walls.

For my MA, I went to Pondicherry University, which cut me off from Jamia for two years. I returned to the campus in 2018 to pursue my MPhil and PhD. I decided to focus on my higher studies during this period, disassociating myself from student organisations and taking a 'retirement' from activism. I had become a serious scholar, focused and eager to go abroad to further my education.

The protests of October 2019 at Jamia changed my views. The

undergraduate students who fought with their whole hearts deeply inspired me. I realized that movements are not only supposed to undo wrongs and eventually change the repressive system, but even before that, they develop better human beings. During this struggle, I felt myself changing — feeling sheer happiness from the revolutionary energy of my juniors — albeit tinged by shame; I questioned myself for standing in the corner. The guilt pushed me towards activity. The contemporary political situation in India made me feel helpless, and I did not expect any significant change in our society. It was the Jamia struggle that pushed me towards hope. One of the friends who called me on the night of our victory asked me about the mood. I told them that the experience had taught me: change is possible — *don't be disheartened since the only thing we must do is fight.*

The most important part of this protest in October 2019 was that we fought to restore the political culture on our campus. I told another friend the same evening that this movement 'gives us a certain kind of political maturity to the campus'. I travelled to many campuses across Delhi — notably the Jawaharlal Nehru University (JNU) — whose students play an enormous role in holding the front line for humanity. The events of October 2019 showed us that every campus has a different socio-political and socio-cultural history and stance toward struggles. The new kind of politics that emerged on campus in October 2019 prepared us at Jamia to struggle against any other sort of political calamity, particularly the protests against the CAA-NRC.

/   /   /

Jamia's mood changed after October 2019. I walked onto the campus in the last week of October, feeling like a part of the campus, feeling that the behaviour of the guards and the clerks would not alienate me from Jamia. A professor had once said to me that the clerks' rooms at Jamia are better equipped than the professors' rooms; that remains true and is suggestive of the administration's priorities. But the day after our victory, I was on the campus of my dreams. For the first time, I downloaded the *Tarana* (anthem) of Jamia and began to like it, and this line became my favourite '*Ye ehle shauq ki basti, ye sarphiron ka dayar*' (This is the sacred sanctuary of dreams, this is the adobe of strong-headed ones)! I felt that Jamia finally seemed like a university. Students seemed closer to each other, with students — who met at the protest — now in touch with students from different departments and faculties. Political discussions filled the hostels and the canteen. Jamia was now *our* campus.

Several universities have come under attack since the BJP government took office in 2014. These included Aligarh Muslim University (AMU), Banaras Hindu University (BHU), Jawaharlal Nehru University (JNU), and the University of Hyderabad (HCU). I had felt scared for Jamia. If we were to be attacked, I felt before October 2019 that the college did not have the political maturity to handle an attack. In my view, the biggest reason is that Jamia is not an integrated residential campus. Unlike AMU, HCU, and JNU, it's not entirely residential and is geographically fragmented. Living on the campus builds a genuine sense of camaraderie.

The victory of October 2019 elevated the mood on the campus. At the end of the struggle, we students produced a press release that captures our seriousness of purpose:

Joint Statement on the Recent Student Protests in Jamia Millia Islamia

On 5 October, 2019, students held a protest demonstration against Israel's participation in campus, following which the proctor, along with guards, manhandled some of the protesting students. Other students immediately reacted and agitated, and an unbiased inquiry into this matter was promised by the proctor. Instead of following up on his promise, the proctor sent show-cause notices to 5 students, including the ones who were manhandled, for protesting against Israel and levelled further false allegations against them. On 14 October, 2019, the students sat on an indefinite dharna. They demanded the withdrawal of the show cause notices, apology from the proctor, disciplinary action against the guards and banning of the State of Israel's participation in the campus. However, no one from the administration came to talk to the protesting students. On the 9th day of the protest, 2000 students marched towards and gheraoed the vice-chancellor office. Later in the day, as the protest continued strongly, the protesters were attacked by goons sent by the administration with the intention of dispersing the protest. Many students were beaten up, and some of them were hospitalized. The Jamia administration has played further foul games, by alleging that the students of English department had entered into a fight with the protestors and that no goons were involved, even though none of the identified attackers has any connection to the English department. In response, Jamia observed its first-ever successful university strike on the very next day, with students coming in large numbers to the vice-chancellor's office in support of the protest. The administrative block was gheraoed again for the whole day by thousands of protesting students. On the 10th day, the administration called student representatives for negotiation, in which the representatives put forward the demands. After the negotiation which went on for 3 hours, the administration agreed to the following demands put forward by the students.

They were:

Legal and strict disciplinary action against the goons sent by the administration.

Withdrawal of show cause notices and no action against the protesting students.

No participation of Israel in the campus.

This victory was achieved by the entire student community

of Jamia and the democratic and progressive voices which stood up with the students against the dictatorial attitude of the administration. It is also the first time an Indian university has agreed to keep out the state of Israel from its programs. However, we must even recognize the fact that there were miscommunications and that a proper democratic process could not be executed in the heat of the struggle. This meant that there was a lack of clarity among some students regarding the action to be taken against the goons. Firstly, the student who was seriously injured has had his hospital expenses taken care of by the Jamia administration.

Further, we assert that there will be no leniency in our attitude towards the administration's gundagardi and that the administrative and legal actions that have been initiated will be followed up by our representatives. The FIR has been registered, and the due disciplinary process should have been undertaken by now. The proctor will be questioned on what action he has taken against the goons who are endangering the safety of the student community. If he has not yet realized it, the proctor will be reminded that he has to serve the students' interests. The struggle against the increasing crackdown on democratic spaces is far from over. It has only begun.

We congratulate all the students of Jamia Millia Islamia for speaking up against this gross oppression. This movement has thrown open the door for more political activities in and outside the campus and brought attention to the glaring lack of platforms in which students can voice their opinions. It has also exposed the hypocrisy of the Jamia administration, which has continuously denied the students their right to union by claiming that it will lead to gundagardi. The fact is that it is the Jamia administration that has always resorted to gundagardi, and shielded gundas by not taking any kind of action against them, and instead focussing on suppressing student voices through surveillance and force. Therefore, it is imperative that we accelerate our fight for student unity and a common pro-student platform.

Long Live Students' Unity!

JOINT STRUGGLE COMMITTEE

(AISA, CYSS, CFI, DISSC, JSF, MSF, Pinjra Tod, SFI, SIO, and Concerned Students of Jamia Millia Islamia)

3. CRACKDOWN

Aaj bazar mein pa-ba-jaulan chalo
dast-afshan chalo mast o raqsan chalo
Let's walk through the Bazar bound in fetters
arms swinging, engrossed in the dance, walk

~ Faiz Ahmed Faiz

Our story begins on 12 December 2019. Students from the girls' hostel gave a call for a march to the main campus against the passage of the CAA bill in the Rajya Sabha. Thousands of girls joined the protest and reached Gate no. 7. Other students joined, and a small meeting turned into a vast crowd. A few girls stood on the boundary wall and addressed the group; they critiqued the government's move and demanded the immediate withdrawal of the CAA. This legacy of courage began with Gerda Phillipsborn. Previously too, in 2018, Jamia girls had staged a protest to relax hostel curfew timings and won. However, this girls' march was historic since it was the first time they had organized such a massive rally. One of the iconic pictures from that day was of four girls raising slogans while playing the *dafli*.

I was not part of this late evening protest because I had already reached home. Once home, I received a flurry of WhatsApp messages: forwarded messages about another march from Jamia to Parliament House scheduled for 13 December; within minutes, I received several digital posters with the same information from different political parties, groups, and organisations; and I also received a banner about an upcoming protest meeting on campus after Friday prayers, organized by the teachers' association. It seemed that there would be both a march to parliament and a protest on campus, although later, it became clear that the march would start after the teachers' association protest meeting.

I had not expected such a big call from the students, certainly not from the teachers' association. The teachers' association is an elected body of the university teachers and operate as a pressure group on behalf of the teachers. I had never seen this kind of activity from the teachers' association. Occasionally individual teachers would take positions in public on this or that issue, but the teachers' association itself neither took a stand with students nor around any common problem. The teachers' association, up until now, had played a minimal and nominal role.

At 2 pm, we reached Gate no. 7. A huge crowd had assembled there. Members of the teachers' association, students, and other organisations were on a small stage just inside the gate. When the meeting began, teachers and students criticized the pattern of government attacks on India's minorities. Thousands of students gathered there in an hour, some inside the campus and some outside. I was happy to see such a crowd at the university; people energized to be concerned citizens. The whole campus echoed with the sound of the *dafli* and slogans, one of which resonates deeply — *ao hamare sath chalo samvidhan bachane nikle hain* (we are out to safeguard the Constitution, come with us). I felt happy to be part of the crowd that was going to save the Constitution. All of us in the crowd believed in democracy: the government had done its part by passing the bill, and the citizens who disagreed with it would play their part in demanding to withdraw the bill.

I was ready to march with the crowd to the parliament and wore proper shoes for the occasion. At the end of the teachers' association meeting, students began to walk toward Sarai Jullena, a neighbourhood north of the university. A friend rang to ask me to wait for her. While I waited for her, the march proceeded and reached the vicinity of the university stadium at the Pataudi sports complex. The nearest landmarks to the campus are Sukhdev Vihar and Sarai Jullena. One road comes to the campus from Sukhdev Vihar and another from Sarai Jullena. The campus is divided by roads into two parts: one part known as the main campus and the other side mainly famous for the names of its buildings. Some people call it the south campus and the north campus. The university campus starts at Gate no. 1 (Engineering) and goes up to Gate no. 4 (the Pataudi stadium, previously named the Bhopal ground).

The protest arrived near Gate no. 1 as I waited for my friend, whose lateness bothered me. I watched the demonstration, impatient to join this exercise of democracy, eager to march to the parliament to make my views known. I called my friend and told her I couldn't wait any longer and set off to join the march. When I approached the crowd, I could not understand what was happening. This atmosphere did not feel the same as the one of slogans and *dafli*; there was something else at work here. I had come in my walking shoes, imagining that we would be chanting and singing as we exercised our democratic rights. But the mood was uglier. I learned that the police had erected barricades at both the lanes of the road and had entirely blocked the passage of the march. Some students had climbed on the barricade and raised slogans. Others climbed onto the pillars at the metro station.

I reached the front of Gate no. 1, which was near the barricade. Students asked the police to allow us to march further. But the police denied our passage. They announced by their wireless loudspeakers: 'You have the right to protest, and you have already done so. Now, go back to your campus'. Students were not prepared to obey the police. We knew our rights. We wanted to exercise them.

After hours of negotiations, the police did not allow us to practice our fundamental democratic rights of protest, enshrined in the Constitution. I could not understand why they would not let us march peacefully. Being a student of political science, I had absorbed my lessons; democracy meant rule by the people, for the people, and of the people. The attitude of the police was the opposite of the democratic spirit.

The action by police created an immediate polarisation between the students on one side and the police on the other. The events that followed stemmed from the action of the police in putting up the barricades, refusing to negotiate with the students, and preventing the students from peaceful protest. The principle and factual division here was imposed on us, and it was: *police vs students*. Later, the government and media would imply that the binary was not between the police and students but between the Muslims and the State. A total fabrication.

The police refused to allow us to march. Our slogans and our requests went nowhere. The students remained adamant about the march, and some students pushed at the barricades, eventually pushing them down. The police beat those who were able to cross the barricade, and then they were detained. We retreated as fast as possible, but the police chased us and fired tear gas. The face of the police was clear: they beat the students mercilessly and wanted to humiliate us. Stopping us at the barricade was not their primary aim.

Some students played Tom and Jerry, winding here and there, throwing *chappals* at the policemen, running back towards the barricade. The police fired rubber bullets and tear gas at these students, injuring many. Violence was one-sided, only from the police (I only once saw students hurling *chappals* at police personnel). I found my senior Vishnupriya Chechi. We held hands to steady ourselves in the scuffle. Suddenly, a school bus appeared, and a student threw a stone at the bus. Luckily the bus was empty. Within seconds, a hundred or so students ran towards the bus and shielded it; they shouted that nothing and no one should be harmed. This incident made me proud. I also ran in front of the bus, though I could've gotten hurt by the stones or the police. I lost track of Vishnupriya Chechi at this point.

The police pushed the students inside the campus's boundary wall. I was already inside the Engineering gate, watching the police fire bullets and gas. Along with hundreds of other students, I ran toward the nearest building. Once inside the building, we washed our faces and our eyes in particular, but it was futile. The whole campus became a gas chamber, and even in the buildings, we suffocated. I arrived near the Department of Physiotherapy, from where I saw the gas and the students running around. There, I saw two girls helping a boy walk because a rubber bullet had hurt him. The girls were furious. The moment we heard the sound of a shot, another bullet on its way, she yelled — *behenchod* (fucker)! This raw and visceral response electrified us. I met some friends at the department and began to look for other friends. Were they safe? Were they detained? Were they in the hospital? We tried to get as much information as possible. Some students were arrested, some beaten, some in hospital.

That evening, we sat and asked ourselves a series of questions. What would happen to our campus? Why was the peaceful protest of 13 December turned by the police into chaos? Why did they transform our beautiful campus into a gas chamber? The protest took place on the roads out of the campus. The police tried to push us away from the road. Once students retreated, why did the police continue to pursue us, why enter the campus, and why attack us on the campus? What made the police turn a simple student protest into a law-and-order issue? Two or three protests against the CAA had taken place on campus, but these did not result in any violence; the only violence that took place was authored by the police when our protest went onto the street.

At 8 pm, I went to the road near the Indian Bank, across from the engineering gate. I saw people banging at the bonnet and mirror of a Maruti Suzuki parked on the side of the road. I rushed there, having understood that these were lumpen guys who were not from Jamia and who were trying to damage the car. I shouted at them and asked them to stop destroying the car, but they had already destroyed a part of it by the time I got there. When I intervened, they threatened me and said they would set the car on fire. Why are you doing this, I asked? They told me that this car belonged to a policeman, so they wanted to damage the car. To stop them, I said the car belonged to a Jamia teacher; but they disagreed. I shielded the car, covering it with both my hands. I searched around for anyone I knew, any other students or guards, but I could not spot anyone. One person came up, asked what was happening, and then joined me. We managed to call a Jamia security guard, who had been in the military and came in a minute. This guard recognized me and sent a message to the control room using his wireless for reinforcements. I was relieved since I would not have been able to fight off these lumpen elements myself.

Jamia's guard-in-charge reached us and tried to call the police. As we waited for the owner of the car to arrive, the goons asked me to come with them around the corner to talk privately. I went along. They seemed to have realized that the Jamia students and staff would not support them, so they asked me — strangely — if I would let them burn the car. They were trying to convince me about the failure of the peaceful route. 'Since the last few days', they said, 'you people have been trying but unable to do anything, which is why violence is needed'. I refused. Jamia guards asked them for their ID cards, at which point they fled.

The guards found the owner of the car, who was indeed a police officer; he was wearing riot gear and walked towards us sweaty. He had been deployed on the other side of the barricade, probably beating the students. He removed his gear and sat in his car but could not move it because of the barricade. I asked the Jamia guards to allow him to park his car inside the university premises. He moved his car into the campus and then returned to duty. That was a powerful moment for me because it showed the democratic commitment of the students: we defended the property of the police officer, even though the police officer was beating us. It was a demonstration of *our* values, values that were not shared by those who sent the police to attack us.

Around 9 pm, the contest with the police came to an end. Students gathered for a meeting on the stairs of the central library.

A friend invited me to come along. The meeting formally took some strategic decisions based on serious inputs from almost every student. The student body decided that our protest had to resume the next day at Gate no. 7, and we agreed that the semester exams scheduled from 14 December should be boycotted. The second decision was taken after rigorous discussion. We felt that it would be difficult to take our exams while other students were injured and detained; we also thought it outrageous that the University administrators did not protest and take any action against the crackdown on the campus and the students. We organized each exam centre to postpone the exams, and I was deployed to the SSB building (one of the vital exam centres).

The following day, I reached the exam centre on time, meeting other students who had come to support the boycott. We raised slogans against the administration's silence at the previous day's incident. We blocked the gate and did not allow students to enter the exam building. Within minutes, the teachers association's office-bearers came to tell us not to boycott the exam, though they did not even take the time to hold a conversation with us even when we tried to initiate a dialogue with them. These teachers' association office-bearers told us that if students could not appear at this place, the university would conduct a separate examination for them. We did not accept this point. Our single-point demand was to postpone the exam from 14 December. Finally, they gave in because they did not have an honest answer to our demand. We waited for an official letter that would authorize the exam's cancellation.

I saw a student wearing a leather jacket who raised religious slogans in the crowd. This slogan had nothing to do with the demand of the students, namely, to cancel the exam and to put pressure on the administration to make a statement. I do not remember the exact slogan from that student. I went up to him and asked for his name. Initially, he did not welcome my presence. When I explained to him that if he persisted in using such a religious slogan at this protest, it would narrow the horizon of our struggle. It was better to raise a pan-Indian slogan, I said. The CAA is not just attacking the Muslim community, but it was first an attack on our Constitution. We must save our constitutional structure and then fight for other issues later. But later, my understanding evolved. I believe that anyone can raise any slogan as long as they are not spreading hatred or offence. And yes, his slogan was neither bigoted nor hateful.

Gate no. 7 became the new epicentre of the protest. Students began to gather there. Some of our teachers came to support us. One of my professors came up to me and asked me how the protest was funded; I said that we don't have any official source; we are collecting Rs 10 and Rs 20 from here and there. She took out Rs 1,500 from her purse and gave it to me. I thanked her and gave the money to one of the office-bearers.

The exam was suspended. The students were free, and then more of them came from across the campus to join the protest. This unity changed the tendency of Jamia's protests to be limited to only a few students. On 14 December, the anti-CAA movement introduced students to one another and introduced all of us to political action on the campus. The crackdown of the previous day pushed us back, but it also gave us the strength to go forward. The protests of 14 December were not restricted to the students. The iron grill gate between the students and the people of Jamia Nagar opened up as people from the locality came to join the protest. Our Gate no. 7 was not only the site where students and some people from the Jamia Nagar area gathered; the eyes of India began to gaze Gate no. 7, and on the protest we held there.

I was standing near the Sociology lawn with my friends. I was not from any political party; I participated in the protest as an individual. Nonetheless, as an older student with political experiences, I provided some assistance, though I mostly kept a low profile. In a couple of hours, the area was full of people, and the speeches began. The speakers talked about the government's attack on the Constitution, the discrimination against Muslims through CAA, and the crackdown on this central university. Many of these themes were new to the people who had gathered at the gate. Most of us were focused on the speaker since the sound system could not project the voices far. My favourite speaker was Pappu Yadav of the Jan Adhikar Party because he belongs to my home state of Bihar, and he always stands for a good cause. I had been part of several protests and listened to thousands of speeches until then. But this was something different since the entire protest comprised people from all strata of society. Though the CAA-NRC was an attack on Muslims, the protests included — Muslims, Hindus, and a range of others. Some of the student leaders who took the microphone were not Muslims. This compositeness gave the campus a positive vibe. It was the most beautiful aspect of this protest.

Amidst this happiness, a friend who is a research scholar in the Arabic department called me and asked me to come to the central canteen. When I reached there, my entire fantasy of compositeness was punctured. The scene was weird. I had walked into a world of political narrowness, where religious identity tried to control the unfolding social dynamic across the campus. I knew that religious slogans — unless hateful, bigoted or divisive — can be a part of public protests. Such slogans could be a reflection of the diversity of our society. The very idea of unity in diversity that we celebrate will be defeated if we do not take along diverse strands of our society. As the anti-CAA-NRC movement reached its zenith, I realized that the faith-based assertion was not only essential but also crucial in mobilizing people. The safeguarding of the Constitution remained the larger goal of the movement for all the ideological strands except the Hindu far-right.

In the years before, Jamia had become a politically paralyzed campus. There were no associations, unions, groups, or political meetings. The credit for this political quarantine goes to former Vice-Chancellor Najeeb Jung. His successor — Talat Ahmed — allowed some democratic space inside the university. Student groups emerged in this period, with various ideologies and cultural processes entering the campus. There was a Gujjar educational organisation to assist Gujjar students, and there was a Kerala cultural society to provide cultural celebrations, with regional fests for Kashmiris and Bihari students. The politics on campus ran the gamut from left to right.

Amongst this efflorescence grew a religious organisation that promoted a form of Islamic politics and values. This was not the only religious organisation on campus, but it was the one that I would meet in the central canteen. Their favourite word is *tehzeeb*, which loosely translates to culture (although, in this context, it is mainly religious culture). This group glorifies Jamia's founder, Mohammed Ali Jauhar, but does so at the expense of other important figures in Jamia's history and the history of India. South Asian society, apart from being religious in every aspect of life, has developed the sensibility of *bhakti* (uncritical adoration) for heroic individuals. Bhakts of Gandhiji do not allow doubts about him, and bhakts for Narendra Modi or the RSS do not permit criticism. Though I must say, there is a massive difference between the bhakts of Gandhi and Sir Syed on the one hand and the bhakts of Narendra Modi and the RSS on the other. When I was in school in Aligarh, I met Aligarh Muslim University (AMU) students who would not allow criticism against Sir Syed Ahmed Khan, the founder of AMU. Like Gandhi or Narendra Modi, Sir Syed ceases to be human in this narrow logic and criticism is treated as a crime. When India's president A.P.J. Abul Kalam, died in 2015, I was an MA student at the University of Pondicherry. A student asked some questions about Kalam's political views, which offended the teacher and other students. I asked the teacher why he admired Kalam. He could not answer me because he was a bhakt without knowledge or understanding. Bhakti, which once might have been devotional love, has now turned into hatred. The rise of the Hindutva forces has contributed to the turning of Bhakti into hatred: bhakts of Hindutva see Muslims as their enemy and drive an anti-Muslim agenda. This has turned minority communities — especially Muslims, but also others like Christians, Dalits and Adivasis — towards creating their own cultural and religious organisations. In the years after 2014, when the BJP came to power, Jamia saw the growth of these kinds of cultural and religious organisations.

I saw that my friend was arguing with people standing near the wall in the central canteen. I understood what was going on when I saw that the walls near the central canteen were covered with religious slogans. It was not merely religious, but it reflected the political assertion of Muslims in a highly charged situation. A student justified the religious slogans on the wall, while my friend argued against any religious slogans (particularly on university walls). I entered the discussion, arguing against using these kinds of slogans. My friend had said, 'this movement is political, so bringing religion is not feasible at all'. I said that the religious slogans have their place, but not here. If we had religious slogans in our protest, I said, they would narrow the horizon of our struggle and alienate those who were not religious. I convinced them to some extent, and they decided to remove the slogans. There was one slogan — about the last messenger of Allah. Some people wanted to remove it, but I disagreed. If Bhagat Singh and Gandhiji can be sources of inspiration, why can't the Prophet also be a source of just leadership? Again, I am not against religious slogans by themselves; I realized later that we could have religious slogans since these are part of our society. I had earlier thought that any aspect of religion in the political sphere was extreme. This is not true. But, yes, I remain against any divisive or bigoted slogans.

After rushing around throughout the day, finally, I saw something very creative, something very artistic and revolutionary going on near the central canteen. Some students, with few resources, were making a wall painting. Seeing this, I thought that finally, something was churning in the Jamia campus from the protest against CAA-NRC: in their own way, everyone was moving the campus forward, everyone was participating in the movement.

I was genuinely interested in the art groups' work, especially those who made graffiti.

Graffiti is an integral part of the revolutionary movement. I was excited to see the artwork on the university walls because Jamia's walls were always out of bounds to such political things. Amongst the group of artists, I saw a girl who would later become the graffiti queen of Jamia. I asked her if I could join, and she welcomed me. I joined the group with some of my friends, and we began to make graffiti on every possible wall that we could reach. The Jamia guards arrived and instructed us to stop. But we did not listen to them and continued to do our work. The security guards informed the authorities, but the proctor probably decided to let the students be. We were too outraged and would not be disturbed by the university officials.

We covered almost every wall of the main campus, including the walls of the library. Our artwork was full of slogans against CAA and NRC. We wrote several revolutionary poems on the walls, including the poetry of Faiz Ahmed Faiz, Makhdoom Mohiuddin, and Rahat Indori. We did some excellent portraits of Bhagat Singh and Ambedkar — the Dalit icon and author of India's Constitution. While painting the walls, I noticed students cross over and look at our art, some even volunteering to join us. A boy came and said, 'I am good at Urdu calligraphy, so please give me something to write in Urdu'. A girl came and asked me if we were getting any funds. I said we don't have any source, so we are crowdfunding. She said she would collect some money from other students. She collected Rs 2,500 and went to buy art supplies for us.

I was always in favour of widening the horizon of the anti-CAA-NRC movement. We did not want the movement to be tagged as Muslim-centric to gain support from across India. With the passage of the CAA, Assam had become the epicentre of the movement. However, due to the incident on 13 December, the media attention shifted to Jamia and away from Northeast India.

We wanted to bring the issues of the Northeast onto the Jamia campus and connect our movement to Assam. I asked the art team leader about this, and she encouraged me to write one line on the wall: *We are with Northeast.* In the context of the anti-CAA-NRC movement, Northeast means mainly Assam. But the movement in Assam was very different from the movement in Jamia. It was xenophobic and racist.

On the late evening of 14 December, students called for a meeting and decided to conduct a march through the locality near Jamia on the next day, which was a Sunday. We were eager to educate the community that lived adjacent to the campus about the issues that had gripped the campus. That day was one of the most horrific days of my life and is taped in our minds like a nightmare in the history of Jamia Millia Islamia. By the evening of 15 December, many erroneous assumptions about the citizenship of Muslims in India became clear. Since I had finished my graduation, I had heard the term 'identity crisis' but never understood it properly; on 15 December, I understood what this term meant. But before I get to the events of 15 December, I want to take you on a journey into my own crisis.

/   /   /

I am an extremely excitable person. To do anything in the name of India's composite culture used to get me very enthused. This fascination with India's composite culture comes from the character of my upbringing. My grandfather would stop my mother from packing non-veg food in my lunch in my childhood. Once I asked him why he was not allowing me to take non-veg food to school. He said, 'Many of your classmates do not eat non-veg, and they might feel bad and incomplete. So, it is better not to carry it to school'. My grandfather taught us a great deal about a range of topics.

We were obliged to listen to him. The most tedious part of

his lectures was his recitation of Urdu and Persian couplets, which he translated for us. His favourite was Iqbal's *Sare jahan se achha*, and others that made me imagine that India was the best country in the world. I would ask him, 'Dada, you always say *hamara Bharat mahan*, but then why is there such bad news reported in the newspaper?' He replied, '*Jab itna bada desh hai to kuchh na kuchh to hoga*' (Unpleasant occurrences are bound to happen in a country as large as ours). This is how he helped me to construct the nation. I believed sincerely in everything he said to me. The rhymes of my nursery were — *Hum sab ek hain* and *We, the people of India*. These beautiful values decorated my childhood and youth — my idea of citizenship where I didn't need to prove myself.

I come from a religious family, a Muslim family that is both modern and conservative. I say all this because the moment you hear the word Muslim, all kinds of unfortunate associations might appear: conservatism, barbarism, terrorism, patriarchy, sexism, and so on. It's part of the anti-Muslim prejudice of Indian society. In these terrible times, with the growth of Hindu right-wing extremism, Muslims are made to feel inferior, backward. I feel compelled to say something like Muslims are just like any other community. But that's obvious. And what makes this strange to say is that I know that Muslims in India share a great deal with other Indians, more than we do with Arabs (someone tauntingly suggested that my Muslim identity connects me to Saudi Arabia). We have little to do with any Arab country in terms of our social, cultural, and political life.

The debate on the idea of India amongst Gandhi, Ambedkar, Nehru, Jinnah, Azad, and others needs to be revived. We need to check our ideas about Bhakti and the composite culture. Gandhi, Nehru, Azad, and other Congressmen believed in composite nationalism, which would include all religions and castes. Dr B.R. Ambedkar, on the other hand, struggled for the rights of Dalits, making a case for the oppression of Dalits and leading the fight against both the British and his own countrymen. Jinnah and his

Muslim League advocated the rights of Muslims, but the Muslims in India were not looking for separate states or merely fundamental livelihood rights; what they sought was — minority rights. With the Partition, Azad and the Congress requested Muslims to stay in India and not go to the newly formed Pakistan; they made the case that a secular India would ensure Muslim minority rights. The majority of Muslims did not go to Pakistan and proudly chose to stay in their homeland. They did not accept the views of Jinnah but thought — like Ambedkar — that the Constitution would guarantee them their rights.

However, in the past few years, Muslims have asked — *who made the wrong decision*? I did not care about this question before 15 December and the anti-Muslim pogrom that followed in Delhi. My inner-self did not raise this question. In Anubhav Sinha's film *Thappad*, the wife asks the husband for a divorce because he's slapped her. She refused to negotiate with him. This *thappad* (slap) compelled her to question everything she previously felt okay about. I had a similar feeling after the horrific incidents of 13 and 15 December.

I will not leave India because India is my land. There is no question about that. But my entire sense of the *Ganga-Jamuni tehzeeb* (distinctive, syncretic Hindu-Muslim culture) was punctured. Before Independence, the Congress drew in Dalits and Muslims and others to forge a united front against the British imperialists. Post-independence, the government — in the name of *Ganga-Jamuni tehzeeb* — neglected the rights of Dalits, Muslims, the Northeast, women, transgender, and so on for the larger goal of nation-building. The Congress accommodated itself to Brahmanical society, failing to uplift those such as Dalits, Muslims, and tribals, who had demanded their rights. Muslims were given some cultural and religious rights, but Dalits were completely neglected. Nonetheless, Muslims and Dalits had a role in society through the accommodative politics of the Indian state.

This limited accommodation ended when the Bharatiya Janata

Party (BJP) brought the RSS agenda to the heart of Indian political life in the 1980s. The BJP's polarising politics based on hatred against Muslims gave a gruesome twist to the accommodative politics of Congress. Muslims like me will never accept being second-class citizens because we were raised believing that India's culture is composite and that the Constitution grants us full rights. But all the words in the Preamble and the Constitution itself began to appear questionable during the BJP government led by Prime Minister Narendra Modi. My crisis is the crisis of a Muslim who begins to feel that composite culture and our citizenship rights are mere illusions.

/ / /

On 14 December, the student organisations decided not to march to parliament. Students agreed that it would be better to educate the people who lived near Jamia about the CAA and the NRC. The area near Jamia houses people from all classes, so we saw their understanding of the CAA and the NRC as vital. Students wanted to use this outreach to gain support for the struggle. We had learned our lessons well!

The students decided to assemble at Gate no. 7 to march into the locality. I do not remember the exact time of the march, but I remember that I reached there a little late. Most people had already gathered there. A large number of people stood in front of the gate. I was unable to see it, blocked as it was by the people. I stood at the end of the crowd, where I waited for a friend to join me. I saw that there was a pink e-rickshaw standing near Batla House. In the distance, I saw two girls sitting on the rickshaw, one of them holding a microphone. They were raising slogans against the barbaric attack of the police on the students and the government for passing the CAA bill. Apart from their slogans, they sang songs to inspire the protestors.

An hour late, the march began in a very peaceful way. We were advised to follow the e-rickshaw. It was a well-organized protest, which did not disrupt the traffic. From Gate no. 8, many of the female students from Jamia joined in as well, the march by now massive. My friend and I joined the rear of the procession. We did not have any duty. Nonetheless, since many people blocked one side of the road, we decided to keep one lane free for traffic. We requested some students to come with us to aid traffic management. From Jamia's Gate no. 7 to the Jamia metro station, we made a human chain as a divider on one side of the road. One side of the road was for the march, and the other was for two-way traffic. Our management was on track. We kept requesting people to remain out of the traffic lanes. Some people wanted to rush ahead, but I put my hand in a gesture to stop them, which was quite effective. One person from the media asked me to pose with that gesture, which I did.

Everything went well till we reached Jamia metro station. By the time I reached that point, the e-rickshaw had already reached the Batla House bus stand. I began to manage the traffic at the metro station because of traffic diversion towards Tikona park. I was stopped there. While informing people about the diversion due to the protest, I saw large numbers of people, including children, run towards us. They wanted to join the march. This scared me. I realized that this would mean that we could have no control over the crowd. I left the job of traffic management at the metro station and rushed toward the Batla House bus stand, but by the time I got there, the e-rickshaw had proceeded towards the Batla House chowk. I was not part of the organizing group for the march, so I was not aware of the planned route.

A vast crowd had by now joined the march. I asked one local person about what was happening and was told that several calls had been made from every colony near Jamia to join the march. I asked him where he had planned to go, but he was clueless. There was no single plan, no leader. The Jamia area had not seen such a huge gathering. There was no experience of anything like this, and no one seemed to know what to do or where to go. The people joined the students but did not know what they would do once they joined our march. This is the lousy fate of Muslim society in India: you cannot find a single leader to lead you for any cause, and you have to wait for someone from outside to come and support you. Another reason for the community's backwardness is that it didn't fight — since 1947 — for political rights, rights that have been refused institutionally, and it now has to fight for its existence.

Relatively poor Muslim neighbourhoods surround our university of Jamia. The vicinity of Jamia has an organic relationship with the university. This relationship has grown naturally. The economy of the area is reliant upon the university. Many university students live in the houses nearby, taking rooms for rent. The university and the surrounding area are often thought of as a Muslim ghetto. During my entrance preparation in JNU, I remember telling several people that I was considering Jamia as an option for my courses apart from JNU and Delhi University. For most of them, Jamia was not an option. Two of them, with anti-Muslim prejudice, said that Papa does not want us to apply to Jamia because Jamia is an Islamic university. Their reaction comes out of this view of Jamia — the university and the locality — as a Muslim ghetto.

In 2008, I was in Class 10 in a school in Lajpat Nagar. On 19 September 2008, the principal of my school called students who lived in Jamia Nagar, such as myself. He told us, 'Batla House has been attacked by terrorists, and there are still attacks going on there, and you must go home right now'. I was then naïve. I told the principal, 'The police should take due action against them'. I was sure that the state should kill anyone who was a terrorist. We boarded the school bus with two teachers who were entrusted with our safety. I reached home within the next few hours. I learned about the attack from every news channel. For me, that was the only political memory I have about that 2008 police attack on Batla House. When I joined Jamia for my graduation, I learned the meaning of *ghettoization* and its relation to Jamia and Jamia Nagar. One of the alleged terrorists in L-18 Batla during the 2008 police attack was a Jamia student. The police failed to prove his involvement in anything to do with terrorism.

I was a Class 10 student when this happened, and I reacted based on my faith in the nation. During this time, I learned about how right-wing forces associated 'terrorism' with Islam and Muslim. Within a few days of the L-18 incident, things started to fray, and I began to ask questions. These questions led me eventually to the idea of *ghettoization*. Since its inception, Jamia was open for everyone, and every Vice-chancellor did their due to make this university the best. During the vice-chancellorship of Professor Mushirul Hasan, there was an attempt to break this image of the Muslim ghetto with an improvement of the academic quality of Jamia, with the introduction of new courses, and with a new sense of the university's relationship to the world. But it was not a complete transformation.

/   /   /

The crowd was not manageable. It was now following the pink e-rickshaw, on which were a few Jamia students, effectively leading this march. Jamia students needed to find a way out of the responsibility for what might happen. Nobody expected such a vast crowd, certainly not those who had organized it. We thought it best to rush forward and inform those who had organized the march about its unmanageability. My friend and I ran from the Batla House bus stand, but we barely crawled forward since there were so many people. We began to push our way forward and reached the middle of the crowd. There, I spotted a face familiar from the October protest. I didn't know them personally, but I had seen them leading the last protest in Jamia. I tried to talk to him but was unable to explain the situation. Then I saw another guy whom I knew personally. I said, 'This campaign march has become so huge. The locals do not know what to do. They are just following us. We should take a call immediately'. We discussed all this at the corner, slightly away from the crowd. He agreed with me. We decided to dash to the e-rickshaw and ask them to divert the march from the proposed route and return to the university campus. We ran and reached the e-rickshaw at Gafoor Nagar, just behind the campus. Due to the enormous rush, it was difficult to talk to anyone, especially those who led the protest. Again, I was lucky. We convinced them and decided to reach Jamia Gate no. 7. The point was to call off the march for the day.

At Gate no. 7, thousands of local people waited for us to lead them to where the government would listen to our voices. Even they did not know where to go and whom to talk to. There was an incredible naiveté in the crowd. The Jamia students had no plan to march to the parliament or the President's House. We only wanted to educate people about CAA and NRC. We knew that this anti-CAA-NRC is a long battle, so we were trying to put some shape to it. Our plan was only for a campaign march, and it was to be only one part of a broader movement. We wanted such small actions to grow organically into a movement. We did not expect the police to thrash us, drawing immediate attention to our movement. We wanted to be part of a long democratic process that would allow every individual to grow.

We followed the e-rickshaw to Jamia's main gate. Very few people knew that the march would terminate at Jamia itself. We shared the information with the organizers of the march. The student leaders understood the situation and agreed with us. Few of them said that they would abide by the decision of the local Jamia residents. Finally, Jamia students decided to call off the march for that day.

When we reached Gate no. 7, we spent an hour discussing this. The local protestors became furious. Since I had convinced the student leaders to call off the march, they asked me to handle the increasingly restive crowd. A student was already addressing the public, and I asked him to continue speaking for as long as possible to keep people engaged. Another student activist came to me and suggested that we ask the two famous faces from the protest of 13 December to call off the protest. I requested them to take the mic and call off the march. They wanted to know why, and I told them that proceeding with such a large crowd could have dire consequences. They agreed, and two of them stood on the rickshaw and called off the protest. After a brief discussion, they said, 'Jamia students are calling off the campaign march here because we have our strategy, and we will march only when we are fully prepared. Those who want to go further are free to go, and others are requested to return to the campus and enter by showing their valid university ID cards'.

The situation became chaotic. Community members began to shout at us. They were furious that Jamia students had called off the protest. With the announcement being made, a vast crowd assembled and waited for a united call from us at the e-rickshaw. We knew that people would be upset, but we had prepared for that. That day — 15 December — was a Sunday, which was a reason why such a large number of people came for the march. The crackdown by the police of the protest on 13 December played on our minds. We knew that the situation was precarious.

We expected our announcement about the postponement to be met with dismay and anger. Our first line of reasoning was that we — students — had to log our protest with the authorities, and we had to follow our rules. We were not prepared for a big march after the crackdown on 13 December. We have to organize ourselves first. We knew that as university students, we had to create a narrative with which to fight the government; we needed clarity and not merely anger. It was an ideological battle, not a physical fight. This thought determined the strategy of the student leaders: we had to do something different than merely acting on our instincts.

We failed to convince the crowd with our arguments. Nobody from the public seemed willing to listen. They wanted us to lead and for them to follow us, but they did not want to follow us by accepting our request to go home. They came up to the rickshaw, outraged. One of them said, 'Why are you scared. You just lead. We will follow'. I told him that as a university, we had to plan, we couldn't decide without a meeting, and that we were scheduled to meet that evening. He challenged us — 'You forgot what happened on the 13 December' — I tried to tell people about the consequences of unclear actions!

After the heated exchange, we began to question our decision to call off the protest. We assembled in the corner and gave it a second thought. Members of one of the student organisations said, 'This movement is not merely Jamia. It is a people's movement. Our party has decided to be a part of the movement'. I said, okay, you could go, but I am not going to be part of this. He said, 'I am not asking anyone to come because the crowd might be unmanageable. Those who want to march can go further'. Whatever followed, for the record, Jamia students were not officially part of the march on parliament or any other building on 15 December. We decided not to participate further in any official capacity.

Most of the students went back into the campus by showing their ID cards. I should say that around 90 per cent of the students went to the campus. Due to the large crowd and the low-frequency microphone, many students did not hear the announcement to end the march. So, they continued with it. At the same time, some others continued marching even after they'd heard the announcement because that's what they wanted to do. They began to march towards some important government buildings. The march was made up mainly of community members and a few students. I went inside the campus with most of the students. Inside the campus, we gathered along with other students who had not left the campus in the first place. The library and the reading room were full of students. In fact, the canteen area was also packed with students who came to the library to sip tea and unwind. It is sad to say that till the 15 December crackdown, most university students did not participate in the protest. They were only focused on their academic work, especially the PhD scholars and others caught up in the rat race of the UPSC examinations.

I was sure of the consequences of the march. I had experienced the police reaction on 13 December and seen how they had attacked the students; what they would do to the local Jamia residents was beyond my imagination. Speaking from instinct and experience, I told my friends and juniors that the police would not allow them even to cross the Jullena red light, and they would chase them to Batla House using tear gas. I was also sure that they would fire inside the campus. I felt the police would attack the crowd, and people would run home, ending the protest. That is also what I *hoped*.

My forecast was proven wrong a few hours later. We sat outside the canteen, going about our day, pondering over managing the protest afresh tomorrow. That's when we got a call that buses had been set on fire at the Jullena red light, and we started to check our phones. I rushed to the main gate, careful to stay inside the boundary wall. I watched the events through the grill. I saw that part of my assumption came true: people rushed frantically towards Batla House. Students from the canteen area came and stood around me. Everybody observed the rush silently. We could do nothing. We continuously scrolled our phones for updates. We saw local people rush back to their homes in the next hour—the smoke from the burnt buses visible from inside the university campus.

The bus burning was horrific. We felt terrible about it. We did not know who had set the buses on fire, but we were sad to see the smoke go up into the sky. The lawn inside Gate no. 7 is known as Ghalib Lawn. It was filled with students, almost as if the entire student body had arrived there. Some said that the whole episode was live on the television channels. I am bad at spotting things on the internet, so I watched it on someone else's mobile. Everyone was watching the live stream on YouTube. I was frustrated with the reporting. Each news channel was busy delivering judgments about the Jamia students. They declared that Jamia students had set the buses on fire. On Google, I typed in 'Jamia news' and saw hate-filled news about Jamia students, claiming they'd disturbed the peace of the city. Some channels were fair, but the bulk was not. They made a complete attempt to suggest that Jamia students are criminals.

We did not know who did what. We were sure that there were a few students from Jamia in the protest. We were worried about what the police would do. We knew that the news reporting was biased, and we knew that this would mirror the views of the police. Even then, I felt that things would calm down. I told my friends that the police would be angry and would lathi-charge the protestors. They would use tear gas to disperse the protestors. I was sure that the police would also throw tear gas into the campus. I assumed that the police would only tackle the residents and not bother with the students since most of us had not participated in the march. They would be able to differentiate between the two. I recalled how when some goons damaged the cars of the policemen on 13 December, it was we students who had saved the car. The policeman said, 'I know that outsiders did these damages. Jamia students will never do this'. My belief in the capacity of the police to retain these distinctions was strong.

We sat near the Ghalib statue, looking at our mobile phones. We had no idea what was going on at the Jullena red light. We tried to get as much information as possible. Our phones started to ring, and we heard something unbelievable. We got calls from the students who were part of the protest. The police had lathi-charged the crowd and beat the protestors brutally. Our friends sent us videos of the police and civilian-clothed personnel beating the protestors. Even those who tried to retreat were beaten. I got scared and did not know what to do. Everyone on campus came to know of the terrible situation. We were sure that since we did not participate in the march and were on campus, we would not be beaten by the police. We did not imagine that the police would enter the campus and thrash us. At most, the police might throw tear gas onto the lawns.

A few students began to shout and ask everyone to walk towards the library. We would take refuge there. One shouted, 'If we gather here, the police might mistake us for protestors. We began to walk towards the library and the canteen lawns. We saw some protestors running back towards Batla House. The police fired tear gas towards them. We watched through the iron grill of our university boundary. Before we knew what was happening, the police fired tear gas into the campus. In no time, the campus was engulfed with the irritating gas. We began to cough and run towards the central canteen. The central canteen area was full of tear gas as well, shells scattered on the ground. Even the canteen workers were running because of the unbearable gas. Despite being extremely spacious, we could not take refuge in the canteen area. We ran towards the library area, which has extensive lawns and gathered on the lawns. All the buildings near Gate no. 7 became suffocating because of the tear gas fired into the campus. Teachers also began to suffocate in the building and left their cabins to gathered in front of the library. Other parts of the campus are not visible from the library, but we could see the smoke rising.

Some guards ran away from their assigned places of duty because of the smoke. Everyone was suffocating badly, while some of us researched online how to bear the smoke. Guards did not allow anyone to go outside the gate, so we walked here and there on campus. We heard the sound of gunfire from the roadside. We were not able to see anything. I sat on the stairs of the main library building with my friends. I saw one of my juniors standing in the corner with her friends. She used to be my student, so I asked her to join our group. I became a sort of guardian or saviour of those standing alone. It felt better to be in a larger group. We stood there for an hour. The sound of gunfire got louder and louder. We were scared and huddled together in the corner.

The main campus has three entry and exit gates. We could not exit because the Jamia guards did not permit anyone to leave. We felt that we could return to our homes in Jamia Nagar once the protest dispersed. Gate no. 7 is the main gate of the campus. It is on the main road, down which the protestors ran. Another gate is near the hostel; it is called the back gate. We also call it the hostel gate because it is near the hostel. Students from the boys' hostel use that gate. The third gate is on the opposite side of the hostel gate and near the university's central library. Opposite this gate is another campus known as the school campus, in which Jamia Masjid is situated. All three gates were closed. We felt encaged. We did not know where to go or what to do.

We were cornered near the library and were unable to move. One student began to shout, saying that the police had entered from the hostel gate and were beating a few students who had come from the hostel. This news spread like wildfire. With the news, shock spread. Everybody began to panic. I saw one girl fall on the steps. Students began to run towards the mosque gate, and because of the enormous rush, the guards opened the gate. Most of the students ran out of the gate. My friends went to the first floor of the reading room because the main library building was closed on Sunday. We did not think of running towards Batla House because the police might catch and beat us. However, some students did run towards Batla House through the small lanes. Panicked students ran helter-skelter.

Someone said that the police had entered from the main gate, gone to the old library building and beat the students there. I was ready to run when I saw the police reach near the canteen. A few students were breaking an earthen flowerpot. I asked them not to throw anything at the police. One of them said, 'They are coming to beat us — throwing stones will keep them away'. I asked him how he could beat a police officer with shards of the earthen pot. Even then, he did not listen to me. That was when I realised that no one seemed to care about anything. In the panic, one guy stopped and told them not to throw the shards. They did not listen to him either. The shards were not able to reach the police personnel. The other guy picked up two branches of a nearby tree, gave one to me, and we started to hit the students to stop them from throwing the stones. We chased them towards the mosque. Whilst chasing them I saw that the police were walking towards me from two sides: one from the polytechnic and another from the canteen area. They were walking casually, not running to chase us.

The library was closed, so we could not hide within it. The reading room was an option. I saw one girl break the glass of the central library building. I rushed to ask her not to break the glass. More students arrived, started banging on the glass, and broke it. (The students broke this glass since they wanted to save themselves; the media mistakenly said that the police broke the glass). They entered the library. There were about 50 girls in the library. I asked them not to go inside because the rooms inside the library were closed. Only the gallery and the hallway were open. In that panic situation, no one listened. They went inside the library. I followed them and asked them to come out because this was no place to hide. They realised that there was indeed no place to hide. All the lights were turned off. Most of the girls gathered in one place. They followed me out, but I don't know where they went afterwards. Two or three of them refused to come outside. I tried to convince them, but they said they would not leave. I ran back to the library gate to escape from the police violence.

The police were at the gate. I had only one option: to rush out of that place as fast as possible. The police were standing on the stairs and ramps at the gate of the library. I ran as fast as possible, but two policemen came and started to beat me as I stepped down from the ramp. I did not stop running and ran towards the mosque gate. I saw police everywhere but ran nonetheless. The gate was open. I paused for a moment to decide where to go, either down the main road to Gafoor Nagar or elsewhere. I checked in both directions. On the right, the road was full of police. On the left, it looked deserted. I chose to enter the Jamia school campus, which was quite dark. After running past the mosque, I went inside the campus and saw hundreds of students gathered there. Some were injured. We hid behind a wall because we did not want the police to see us. That was the only part of the campus where the police did not launch tear gas. This was soon to change.

While we hid behind the wall, the police came near the mosque and fired tear gas into the mosque. The Imam saab asked the police not to fire tear gas into the mosque and asked the students to go home. He repeatedly announced on his mic, 'The mosque comes under my jurisdiction, and the university has nothing to do with it, so please do not enter the mosque premises. Students should go home'.

We were stuck there for thirty minutes. The police had overrun our campus. Hiding behind the wall, we called friends to learn about what was going on in other parts of the campus. I called a friend who was with me at the library stairs before the police entered the campus. He said he was hiding on the first floor of the new reading room, the PhD section. He said, 'when panic set in, you got lost somewhere, and I was with four girls. We tried to find a safe place. I found the PhD section gate open, and the rest was closed. So, we came here'. I asked him what was going on. He said, 'we switched off the lights and hid under the table, and the police are doing something downstairs because we can hear students shouting'.

The school campus is visible from the road. There is only an iron grill that divides the campus from the streets. The police saw us standing peacefully and nonetheless entered the campus. We knew we had to save ourselves. We did not know where to go. At the rear of the campus is the fine arts department. There is one guard there. He showed us the way out through the boundary wall. He said, if you jump this wall, you will be in the graveyard; from there, you can get to Batla House. We followed the guard's instructions and reached the Balta House chowk.

While I hid in the school building, my friends were in the first-floor reading room. At that time, only the most horrific things were happening on the ground floor. We got several WhatsApp videos — each ten to fifteen seconds long — which showed the police beating up students, the place filled with smoke. Later we would learn more about this incident.

The police targeted the students with violence. They came onto the campus to beat us, not to disperse us. I thought that the police had come to disperse the students. We had already been dispersed. Those of us on campus were not endangering anybody. When they arrived, we ran and hid. Yet, they chased after us and beat us. I can understand if we had been on the road or if we had been in the act of rioting and then if they beat us. But why beat students in the library? The police turned the entire library into a warzone. It seems like they were dealing not with students but with hardened criminals.

The police entered both reading rooms. The new reading room is part of the central library building, where we were all initially standing. The guards and the staff locked the entry gate of the new reading room. First, the police went to the washroom near the new reading room because some students had locked themselves into the toilets. The police broke the soft plywood doors and beat the students mercilessly, and made them sit in one place within the library. Then, the police went to the gate of the reading room, which was locked by a grill gate. There was a gap between the iron bars, so they threw tear gas into the reading room. The reading room was filled with students. The tear gas came in from both sides, making the place unbearable. The students had no option except to suffocate inside the room because the police were at the door. Finally, the police broke the lock, went into the new reading room, and hit students with their batons. Some students hid under the large central table. Other students took refuge inside the bathroom, in the storeroom, in the electricity room, and elsewhere. Most of the students picked up by the police were made to sit in one place. Those who had been sitting in front of the library were severely injured.

One of the oldest buildings on the campus — the old reading room — is near the main gate, visible from the road. The room is always full of our most studious students, who come when the space opens in the morning and leave at 2 am (even later during examination time). These are the students sitting for the UPSC or diploma students; they are the real *padhai-likhai* (studious) students. These students occupied the building. Many other students ran in there to escape from the police. There are several rooms in the building, and the students locked themselves inside these rooms. When the police started to bang on the door, students placed a heavy table to barricade themselves. The police broke the old wooden door, went inside, and beat the students. No one inside the building expected this kind of behaviour from the police! They even broke the CCTV cameras in the rooms. There are two small rooms in the old reading room reserved for MPhil students. These two rooms are tiny, with one entry and exit. Other reading spaces are pretty big, with many students studying there. In the small rooms, there is no room to run. The police entered these tiny rooms and beat the students as if they were animals. They hit the students on the head, on the hands, in their eyes, and so on. The students who were merely there to study were beaten.

The students were removed from the reading rooms and taken outside to sit on the floor. Later, video clips of this violence were posted on YouTube.

The police went to another section of the library, including the girl's section and beat up more students. Some students hid in the washroom, but there was no safe place that day; they were beaten and thrown on the floor. A student, also attacked in the bathroom and left bleeding on the dirty floor near a urinal, lost his eyesight. Police took the other students outside by the gate and to the nearest police station. The most severely injured students were taken to AIIMS, where they received treatment. The rest, many of whom were grievously hurt, were held in the police station without medication. Later, I met two students who were treated at AIIMS. One told me he was bleeding from the forehead while the other bled from several places. They tore a handkerchief into pieces and covered their wounds. A student, whose hands were broken, was taken to the NFC police station — and made to sit on the floor in that condition through the night.

The police crackdown came in three phases. First, the police fired tear gas and cornered us near the library. The police had already dispersed us, so there was no need to enter the campus and beat us. But this is what they did. The second phase was when the police thrashed the students. The question lingers: why did the police enter the campus and attack the students when most had not participated in the march? Having beaten students they found, the police then went looking for students who were hiding, especially in the library but also in other buildings. The police did not beat all of them; they ordered them to sit at one place as if they had been arrested and then asked them to stand with their hands up. They were then made to walk where the police wanted them to walk. The police then allowed these students to evacuate — which is the third phase. These students were allowed to go towards Jullena with their hands up. Some students were scared because they had already seen the videos. The police assured them not to be afraid and told them to march in a single file through the gate. The police crackdown ended.

Around 400 students were injured on 15 December 2019. One student lost an eye, and another had both hands broken. A video of police beating up five or six students on Mathura Road went viral. Most of them were girls, hiding in a building parking area. It was vicious. This video circulated everywhere and shook the world.

4. AFTERMATH

Hum to jaise wahan ke thei hi nahin
be-aman they aman ke thei hi nahin
Now it seems I never belonged there
I was always shelterless, never belonged to that place

~ Jaun Eliya

The image of the university in India has sustained significant damage since at least early 2016. In January 2016, there was an attack on Hyderabad Central University (HCU) as part of the reaction to the institutional murder of the Dalit scholar Rohit Vemula. A month later, there was a sedition case placed on JNU Student Union leader Kanhaiya Kumar and others, accusing them of raising anti-national slogans. In December 2019, Aligarh Muslim University (AMU) was attacked before the Karnataka elections over a portrait of Mohammed Ali Jinnah that hangs in the university student union hall. These attacks damaged the image of the university. The universities were labelled as anti-national, *lafde wali jagah, deshdrohi* university, and so on. Parents became reluctant to let students study at these prominent public universities.

I felt lucky. I used to say to my friends, 'Jamia did not come under this kind of attack. Even the government knows that Jamia is a small university with less capacity to influence people. That is why the government does not bother with us. I knew that if such an attack occurred, the students at Jamia would not have the resources to manage it. Jamia is different from Aligarh Muslim University, Hyderabad Central University, Jawaharlal Nehru University, Jadavpur University, and Pondicherry University. These universities have a substantial residential campus, with thousands of students in residence who can stand up to defend their campus. They are also rich with active student political life, with several social and cultural platforms that have bound students into one thread — into a campus society. Jamia is different. Most students do not live on campus. At some point in the evening, we go home. The campus did not have a rich political life, nor does it have a social life that attaches students into one thread. Students merely attend classes and then spend time in the canteen before returning home.

After the crackdown of 15 December, I slipped through the wall of the graveyard and reached the Batla House chowk. It is known as a place where you can buy sumptuous food till late into the night. We used to sit in the library's reading room during our exam times and then leave famished near 2 am to get food at the Batla House area. It is known for its hustle-bustle, round the clock. But, as I entered the area, Batla House was desolate.

Poets easily take the measure of pain. I have a habit of reciting poetry when something hits me hard. That day, when I reached Batla House, the famous Mirza Ghalib couplet came to me:

> *Koi umeed bar nahi ati*
> *koi surat nazar nahin ati,*
> *age ati thi hal-e-dil pe hansi*
> *ab kisi bat par nahi ati*
> I see no hope in the living,
> I see no solution in sight.
> Earlier, I scoffed at the dilemma of my heart
> but now nothing amuses me.

I felt helpless. I felt that the Jamia community was helpless. I was all alone and unable to help my friends. I did not know that the police had evacuated the campus. I had no idea who was where, whether the injured had been to the hospital or the *thana* (lock-up). I received hundreds of messages from everywhere: someone stuck in a building, someone jumping over a high wall, someone in a lathi charge, someone locked in the washroom.

I felt helpless due to the situation of Jamia. In other universities, the students stay on campus and develop a culture of their campus, which creates a legacy amongst graduates. We are thrown away from our campus after a few hours. We could not save our campus. That evening, we watched videos of the police breaking up chairs and tables inside the library. They broke everything: furniture, windows — students' bones! I was filled with anxiety. I asked, 'will they allow us to function as a university again?'. What we had witnessed in the past few hours was extraordinary for the university and its students. Later, the University authorities would say that the police violence led to damages that cost Rs 2.66 crores.

I walked along the roads to Batla House, unsure where I was going, looking continuously at my phone. I got several calls from people who know that I am always on campus. They inquired about my safety. Just imagine: we are students of a central university situated in the capital city, and people from far away are concerned about our safety and security within our campus. I got a call from a junior who asked me for my exact location and then disconnected. Within a few minutes, he came and stood in front of me and took me to his room. I followed him, using my phone. We reached a small *gali* (lane) and then entered a small building. I entered his student flat on the fourth floor; it was completely disorganised and had a dirty kitchen. He had given refuge to other students, including a female student. The cluttered room gave me a sense of nostalgia. Looking at the faces of other students who had taken refuge there — deeply shook me. Everyone looked traumatised. They were clueless about what was going on at the campus. They were focused on their phones — desperately trying to reach friends and relatives — trying to learn what was happening at the campus.

We were far from Jamia, but still, we heard the sound of firing. I was scared about the possibility of a communal clash. We greeted each other with sad faces and shared our stories.

Our phones filled up with forwarded messages and videos. Every minute we were getting bad news. The news channels gave us an idea of the extent of police brutality. Huddled together, we tried to support one another. While most students were trapped in the dark building across campus — others were detained or hospitalised. The police operation had finished. The news trickled in slowly. Many students were wandering on the roads because they did not know where to go. Everyone was scared to return to the campus. When police were beating people, they scattered but did not know where to take shelter. They remained in that disoriented state. Many had lost their shoes in the melee. Girls did not know where to go, unsure about taking refuge in friends' rooms. Our first job was to accommodate each student, especially those wandering on the roads. We chose it as our primary task to guarantee the safety of the students. We began to call everyone we knew and checked their whereabouts, finding places for them. While checking, we found that two or three students were locked in a dark electricity supply room. They had to break down a dilapidated university wall during the crackdown and run through a residential colony to eventually find refuge in the electricity supply room. Some students hid in the washroom through the night.

While we struggled to find safe places, something *beautiful* happened which brought us some solace. We received several addresses and phone numbers in forwarded messages from people who volunteered to accommodate the students. We were not alone. I think this was something incredible. In a few minutes, we got the addresses of hundreds of people who opened their doors to give the traumatised students shelter. These messages read: *my house is open, and this is my address, and I can accommodate six students.*

Teachers and seniors also called from far off; fortunately, we could accommodate all the students near the campus.

Some of the news we received was false. How do you deal with this? We didn't want to believe all of the information received on WhatsApp groups. We spotted several images which were not from Jamia but that the news claimed was Jamia. We saw on Facebook that one student had died in the crackdown. That news froze us. We decided to verify it. People told us they had heard it from this WhatsApp group or that Facebook page. Eventually, we tracked down the origin of the story. We called the person, and he said, 'I did not say anything to anyone because I do not have information about someone's death'. Even though we broke the story and said that this was fake news, it had already affected many people. Many people believed that there was a death at Jamia. Such fake accounts have an impact. It was a fake story that drew the UP Police onto the AMU campus. We know what happened there. We spent our time checking fake news and countering it.

Ashutosh Tiwari, who hails from Deoria (Uttar Pradesh), got a call from his father. His father must have called to ensure his wellbeing. 'You are the one who voted for this government, so don't expect my well-being now', he yelled into the phone. This minor phone incident brought a smile to our sad faces. We got information that the students at AMU had begun to protest in solidarity and that people in Shaheen Bagh had blocked the road. We heard that students from JNU called the police headquarters at ITO to protest the violence; they demanded the immediate release of the students. We could not focus on what had begun to happen at AMU, Shaheen Bagh, and ITO. We were too busy settling people and checking on others.

At midnight, my friend went downstairs and brought us some food. We took some rest. I went to my aunt's house, and she insisted I stay with her. While working to expose the fake news, I had missed many calls. I called them back from my aunt's house. My friend Arushi Singh called me from Taiwan. She was a Masters from Jamia and then went to Taiwan on a scholarship. 'What have they done to my university? Why are they breaking my beautiful campus' she asked? I was speechless. I did not have an answer. I could not calm her down. My friend Pratimah Yadav, who had completed MPhil from Jamia and was pursuing PhD from IIT Madras, called. She was crying and asked how I was feeling. 'The good thing is that we are not scared at all', I told her. 'Police lathis make us fearless'. I could not sleep. I found out via WhatsApp that some students went to the police headquarters. I called a friend from JNU, Apoorva. She was at ITO. She told me that a few delegates from JNU had gone inside the police headquarters and had demanded the release of all students. She suggested I get some sleep and promised she'll update me if there was any progress.

I fell asleep at 3 or 4 am and woke up only when a friend called at 8 am. My friend asked me to go and check on the students who had been admitted to the Holy Family Hospital. On 16 December 2019, I walked through the cold morning air from my aunt's house and reached Jamia. I saw reporters from different news channels. A student, shirtless, was crying in front of the gate. A media person asked him to put on his clothes because she felt terrible for him, but he refused to wear anything in the chill of the winter. I went to Holy Family Hospital to check on the students without talking to anyone. I was denied entrance at the gate. I asked the receptionist about the whereabouts of the students. She told me that most students had been discharged at night, and a few were in the ICU. Apart from that, she did not say anything.

As I walked away, a TV reporter asked me, 'are you a Jamia student?' and when I said, 'yes', she asked me what I was doing at the hospital. The question shook me. I asked myself this question. Why was I looking for my friends in the hospital and the police station? I should be with them in the canteen and the library. The state had imposed this on me.

When I walked back to Jamia, I saw the massive deployment of the police and paramilitary force near the wall of the Holy Family

Hospital. It was at the point where the Jamia campus began. When I reached the university campus, I saw many people from Jamia Nagar on the road. They were talking to the media. There were hardly any university students.

I felt broken. I didn't feel like doing anything. I think everyone felt this way. I got a call from a journalist with the *Hindustan Times*. She wanted to visit the library. I went to the mosque gate to ask the guards. I went in with her. I saw a group of media persons already there. They were reporting in their typical fashion. We entered the library, and whatever we saw was menacing and tormenting. The furniture was broken, the windowpanes smashed, the CCTV cameras smashed, blood splattered on the stairs. I began to cry. The journalist comforted me and offered me water. She took photographs and notes and asked me to take her to the new reading room. The thought of seeing it made me anxious, so I declined. We could not walk around the campus as it was locked down. No one was allowed on the campus. All the examinations were cancelled, and the students had been asked to vacate the hostels. Most of the students started to leave for their homes. When the girls left the hostel, the warden asked them to sign a blank paper, but they refused. It was pathetic to watch the students walking from their hostels with their bags, leaving the campus without finishing their exams. We were being thrown off our campus. The university was declared closed till January.

A senior who joined Ambedkar University (Delhi) as a faculty member called me. She came to Jamia, and I met her on campus. She told me that the teachers' body of Jamia and teachers from all the universities based in Delhi were going to hold a protest march. I joined it and was amazed to see so many university professors at such a gathering, many for the first time. The procession began at the Ansari Auditorium to the Engineering Auditorium via the FTK CIT, Hygienic Café, and the Physiotherapy Department. The detritus of the crackdown was everywhere. I went to meet someone at the Hygienic Café and saw that it was destroyed. The door to the History Department had been broken. The procession went to the university auditorium. All the teachers held placards thanking colleges that had stood with Jamia. One professor held a placard that read: Thank You, Pondicherry. This brought a smile to my face.

At this point, my friend's brother called me, asking me about his well-being; he'd been my undergraduate classmate since 2012. Up until then, all the people had not been traced. Many had left for home without informing their families. We had assumed that if so and so was not on campus, then they had gone home. It was impossible to track everyone. I saw my friend on 14 December. We had a heated debate over a cup of tea. I became angry when he said, 'to pose with the JNU type of protest'. I asked him what 'type' this would be. He said, 'you should give classes on CAA and NRC to people'. I asked him to come and initiate this and be part of the protest. But he didn't. He went back to the reading room. I didn't know where he went. Some student leaders asked me to check the hospital list. I couldn't track all the hospitals. We were each assigned a hospital; I was assigned to the Holy Family Hospital. I eventually found out that he'd been severely injured and admitted to AIIMS, from where he'd been discharged, and left for his rented room. Hearing this, we rushed to his see him.

We, three friends, reached his room with juice and fruits, the formalities that *bade* (elders) would do. I was not in favour of all this, but still, we took something. He lived on the fourth floor of a tiny building in Jamia Nagar. He was sitting on the corner of his bed. We saw stitches on his forehead and just above his nose. I tried to cheer him up, but he wanted to tell us what had happened to him. He had told this story many times since the morning, but he wanted to tell it again. It was, one of us said, 'a coping mechanism for him'. He said:

I was studying in the MPhil section of the library when I learnt about the police crackdown; I went down to see the commotion. I saw the entrance gate of the library was closed, and I came back to the M.Phil. section and asked everyone to calm down. But when the police started banging on the door and throwing tear gas from the glass window, the students ran out from the ground floor and started running here and there. We locked the wooden door and placed a huge table in front of the gate. Police broke down the door, entered that room, and started beating everyone with their sticks. I hid in a corner and put a carton on my body, but the police saw me and started beating me. I said to the police — *Bhagwan ke lie mujhe chhod do* (For God's sake, spare me) — the police taunted — *Allah ke nam pe bol* (Beg for mercy in Allah's name) — and in-between all this, they struck me with a stick on my forehead. I started feeling something near my eye, and then I felt blood flow on my face. Soon after, the police asked me to walk in line and sit in front of the library building where other students were already sitting. After some time, a few policemen came and started pushing us towards the main gate. There was a jeep waiting, and they started throwing us in that like luggage. My shirt was drenched with blood. While holding my wound with a small handkerchief, I noticed another guy bleeding and trying to stop his blood with his hand. Blood was flowing from his head, and he did not have anything to soak the blood, so I tore my handkerchief into two parts and gave one part to him. Finally, the jeep started moving, we didn't know where we were going, but I heard the policeman was instructing someone to go directly to AIIMS.

That's how he ended his story. He said that he would go home soon because he was too traumatised. When someone knocks on the door of his room, he feels that it is the police banging on his door, and soon they will break the door down. He kept his torn handkerchief and showed it to everyone. Another set of guests arrived, and we took our leave.

/   /   /

On 16 December, we saw several people gathered at Gate no. 7. It soon became the centre stage of the protest against the CAA-NRC. Along with Jamia, Shaheen Bagh gained momentum in the movement against CAA-NRC. On the night of the crackdown, people from Shaheen Bagh blocked the road that linked Noida to Delhi. They held a 24-hour protest, which soon became permanent and iconic.

Thus far, the Jamia students did not organise any protests because most of them had left for their hometowns. A few students were in Delhi, but there was no way to connect us to an organisation. Our campus was locked. We were not able to come together. We had no space for building anything. Primarily local people began to gather outside Gate no. 7. A significant media presence attracted people there. We felt helpless and left out.

On 17 December, I stood near Gate no. 7, a little away from the crowd with some friends. We were there to see the protest but were not a part of it. While standing there, a few teachers walked towards Gate no. 7. We asked them where they were going. 'We are going for a teachers' association meeting', they said, 'to discuss the situation'. We asked them to invite us because we had nothing to do. They agreed, so around 10-15 students went to the teachers' association office. The meeting became one of the teachers' association and the students. We made two demands: that the campus be opened and the protest on campus restarted. The teachers' association responded, 'Protest must start, and you will have to come together regardless of every kind of difference, be it personal or political'. They said that since the teachers' association is an elected body of teachers and not a student group, 'we will not be able to stand on the road like the students, but we will support students in every step of the way'. We emerged from the meeting and gave a call for another one. We invited students from every political organisation. Teachers' association suggested that we unite at every level and club, including other associations. A final meeting was called, which was to be attended by students from every political party, independent student activists, and every officer bearer from every elected body.

I was not part of any political organisation, so I decided not to attend any formal meeting for the protest. I learned from my friends, who were at the meeting, that they had formed a committee to manage the protest ahead. It was called the Jamia Coordination Committee (JCC). 'JCC is an independent organisation; its structure consists of 2-3 members from every party, and independent activists will be part of JCC. They will take all the decisions, and its followings will be purely democratic', they said. The JCC formed a WhatsApp group and issued a press release.

Date: 18 December 2019

Time: 12 am

A meeting was held on 17th December 2019 to form the "Jamia Coordination Committee" (JCC) to involve different stakeholders including students, teachers and alumni of Jamia Millia Islamia. In the light of recent police brutalities on 13th December and 15th December, the committee has been formed with the agenda of responsibly organizing non-violent protests and sharpening the struggle against the unconstitutional CAA and NRC.

We condemn the nationwide atrocities inflicted upon the people who were protesting against this law, which seeks to make a whole community powerless. We also specifically condemn the brutalities unleashed upon Jamia Millia Islamia, Aligarh Muslim University, Delhi University, Seelampur, Zafrabad and on protest sites across the country. Academic institutions are responsible for upholding the idea of egalitarianism and be the bastions of dissent and debate, and JMI and AMU are being targeted for doing exactly this. The two institutes became the ground for strong protests against CAA and NRC. It was not simply the students of the universities who were attacked, but the universities themselves. Normalcy must be restored in these two universities, but normalcy does not mean enforced peace and silence. Our voices will continue to rise in protest against injustice.

We understand that the struggle is a long one and hence we have resolved to fight until CAA is revoked and NRC is rejected, in a university-wide coordination. The protests will continue, and our future course of action will be duly announced. We appeal to the people to join us in the struggle against CAA and NRC.

AAJMI, AISA, CFI, CYSS, DISSC, JSF, MSF, Pinjra Tod, SFI, SIO, Khudai Khidmatgar and all concerned independent activists.

The JCC divided the students into teams for work on media, stage, guests, speakers, crowd control, food, finance, and so on. Students were assigned tasks and asked to report for a daily meeting on campus. The JCC began to organise the protest. This is how the protest returned to Gate no. 7. There were several marches, public meetings, and celebrations. Every day new things came up at the protest. It was a kind of festival, where people set up counters on the roadway and displayed posters and pamphlets, messages and photos. These counters had names like: Read for Revolution, Write for Revolution, Art Gallery, Study Circle, Lecture Series, Photo Gallery, Tea Counter. The walls were covered with graffiti. These became a crucial attraction. At 10 am, JCC assigned people to come and block one side of the road to set up a stage. In the afternoon, the protest would become a mass demonstration. The speakers would come at noon and stay till 7 pm. Not far, Shaheen Bagh also blossomed. It became famous because of its all-women leadership. Students from Jamia also participated in Shaheen Bagh. After 7 pm, everybody would go to Shaheen Bagh in the evening.

Later, the Shaheen Bagh protest became a 24×7 sit-in protest.

The protest began on 15 December 2019 and lasted until 24 March 2020, for three months. We discontinued the sit-in and dismantled the site due to the outbreak of COVID-19. The students followed the government order and left the protest. The police came and defaced our artwork. They dismantled everything we had built there.

On 30 January 2020, the 72nd death anniversary of Mahatma Gandhi, Jamia students initiated a March from Jamia to Rajghat to pay homage to the father of the nation, who had fought against communalism. The police had camped near Jamia alongside the paramilitary forces; they kept a vigilant eye on the protest. They were prepared with barricades, putting them up on both sides of the road; the police would sit at the barricades. When students planned a protest, the police put a heavy barricade to prevent it, and the riot police would standby. Our march from Jamia to Rajghat started peacefully from Gate no. 7 with slogans and the beating of the *dafli*. We reached Gate no. 1, at the edge of the Jamia campus. I was at the back of the protest.

The police had barricaded the exit. When I reached Gate no. 1, I got a call from a friend, who asked me about the firing incident near the protest. I freaked out and scolded her for spreading rumours. On 16 December, a newspaper reported that two Jamia students had been shot; this report was false. That was why I reacted in this way. The protest was not moving. I was suspicious. I knew that the police would not let us proceed beyond the Holy Family Hospital. My friend called me back, 'there was firing at the protest, and a bullet hit one student. I have seen people rushing to Holy Family'. I asked her how she got these details. She said that she was in the hospital for surgery on her foot. By the time I disconnected the call, everyone seemed scared. The news was in the air.

The video was already viral. I saw it on my phone. A young boy with a gun fired at one of the students while this boy chanted, '*Jai Shri Ram*' and 'Police Zindabad'. He opened fire while saying,

'*Kisko chahiye azadi? Main dunga azadi*' (Who wants freedom? I will give them freedom). The bullet hit Jamia student Shadab Farooq who was trying to stop him. We received several videos of the shooting. It was clear that the boy had a gun, yet the police did not stop him. After he fired his gun, he rushed towards the police.

Shadab was shot in the hand. The injury was mild. When the bullet hit him, friends held him and took him to Holy Family Hospital. The police did not allow Shadab space to walk through the barricade even though he was bleeding. I still wonder why the police did not assist an injured person. The shooter was arrested by the police, who said he was a juvenile and slapped him with an attempted murder charge. How did a schoolboy get a gun and walk up to shoot people? What kind of society had we become? A terrible contagion had begun to spread through our culture. Later, a person would shoot at the Shaheen Bagh protest site. And then we got the violence in North East Delhi. I read that when the Shaheen Bagh shooter was released from jail, he was given a grand welcome by his friends, followers, and political functionaries.

Exams that had been postponed in December were now slated for February. The slogan *Study and Struggle* resonated. It means that we must study and struggle at the same time. Students were busy with their preparations. They went to protest in the day and studied for the exams at night. On 2 February 2020, as people protested at Gate no. 7, two unidentified bikers came and fired shots near Gate no. 5. I was not there at the time, but I saw the reaction on social networks. One post by a girl shook me: 'Studying for my exam with keeping an iron rod and cricket bat under my bed. Can't ask for a better night to study. #firing@Jmi#gate no5'. No one was injured.

The JCC called for another march on 10 February. Police stopped us just before the Holy Family gate at the same spot. I was always at the end of the protest. I found a comfortable spot near Ashok Chai, which the police had once more asked to shut down; I was sitting with some friends, giving *gyan* to them. After a while, I saw a few students running towards the university. I asked someone what was going on and found that the police were pushing people back once more. Running had become common for us. I got a call from a journalist, 'is there any lathi charge at Jamia?', and I said, 'no, there is no lathi charge. Students are running as part of the "tom and jerry" situation'. I got another call, asking me to check out what was happening. I did not bother, knowing full well that this kind of 'tom and jerry' game is typical between the police and the protestors. But then I saw some students being taken away in an e-rickshaw; they seemed unconscious. I thought it might be due to suffocation. I remained seated with my friends. Around 6 pm, we went to have tea on the campus and learnt the whole story.

It was shocking. As the students marched, the police attacked them, hitting the boys and girls below the belt. Police were on both sides of the barricades, and they deliberately struck the students where it would hurt with their boots, knee guards, and batons. These students were severely injured, many had to be taken to hospital. There were pictures of this incident on Facebook. The following day, I went to the hospital to meet the injured girls. One 17-year-old enrolled in the first year was in bed, her mother crying beside her. I managed to console her, but she was terrified. I called one of my teachers and told her the whole story. She went and met the girl's mother and assured her that there would be no retribution against her daughter. I met the mother several times again.

These were the stories of sadness and pain, happiness and revolution.

5. SHAHEEN BAGH

Hizabe fitna parvar ab utha leti to achchha tha
khud apne husn ko parda bana leti to achchha tha
Better, if you could pull down the hijab of shyness, now;
better instead, if you could make your boldness a veil

~ Asrarul Haq Majaz

14 December was a historic day for women across the globe, especially for Muslim women. It is not usual for women — irrespective of their religion, caste, or class — to be on the road unless they have been organised through various channels. I have witnessed many protests, and the presence of women has usually been minimal. Shaheen Bagh was a different story. The protests of Shaheen Bagh reveal a new movement in India, with women in the lead. The highlight of the protest was that it was led by women, managed by women, and not for a women-specific issue. In other words, the uniqueness of the protest is that it was not strictly for women's issues, but it was under the leadership of women.

The protest at Shaheen Bagh became a platform. It was not limited to CAA-NRC but expanded to more than that. Leaders from across the country visited Shaheen Bagh to demonstrate their solidarity. Various movements joined in at Shaheen Bagh, which became a platform for dissent, for protest, for condolence, and for solidarity. Shaheen Bagh reached out to Kashmiri Pandits, who had completed thirty years of their exodus; the protestors paid homage to the martyrs of the Pulwama attack by observing one-minute silence; they remembered the suicide of the farmers; they paid heartfelt tribute at the death anniversary of Rohit Vemula.

On 15 December, when I was mentally and physically displaced, the after-effects of the crackdown weighing on me, I tried to ignore the news. On the night of the crackdown, I felt that everything was over; our democracy was tarnished. What I had seen with my own eyes on 15 December ended my optimism. *What will happen now*? That was my only thought! There was no answer. Deep down, we wanted the university to be spared from any political retribution. It was merely limited to restarting my studies. *Movement gaya bhad me, bas university khul jaye* (Forget about the movement, let the university resume). That was my thought during the horrible night of 15 December.

That night, while I slept in my aunt's house, I saw some messages about the police crackdown at Jamia. I felt that no one would bother about this attack since we are a government-funded university, and on top of that, it is also considered a minority institution. Who is concerned about our university and the beating of mostly Muslim students? Why would anyone — let alone the media — be bothered with the beating of 1000 students, injury of 400, the detention of 50-100 students and damage to the university infrastructure? Social media, however, played a key role. Short videos captured by students of the crackdown went viral. Within a few hours, these horrific visuals helped Jamia students bring attention to what had happened to our campus. During our three days, I would discuss a theory of these *visuals* with my friends: No matter what forces are working against you in the name of physical and abstract, if you have visuals, your narrative will be compelling.

To illustrate with an example — in July 2016, some Dalits were accused of skinning a dead cow in Una, Gir Somnath district in Gujarat. Cow vigilantes assaulted them because they accused them of killing the cow. Four of the Dalit men were stripped and tied to the back of the car and beaten mercilessly. The assailants made a video that went viral on social media, later resulting in state-wide protests. Television channels would show the video over and over again. Before this, I had never seen such a bare truth about anti-Dalit violence on national television. This affected people. Similarly, a twenty or thirty-second video of the attack on the Jamia library impacted people. It showed the police brutally beating the unarmed and innocent students, many of them crying for help. By the night of 15 December, these visuals appeared on television. The reaction was apparent. People were upset.

On 14 December, a few women went onto the road at GD Birla Marg (also known as Kalindi Kunj Road) to protest against the CAA. This was a small protest. After the attack on Jamia, the protest became huge. People from Shaheen Bagh, especially women, gathered on the road that links Delhi to Noida and blocked it. They erected a stage on the road, the protest site extended to a kilometre. This became the epicentre of a 24-hour sit-in. It would last until the police vacated it due to COVID-19 on 24 March 2020, making it a 101-day protest.

Shaheen Bagh emerged out of the crackdown on Jamia on 15 December (as well as the crackdown that same day on Aligarh Muslim University). It became a symbol of the movement. Those days I saw one WhatsApp status: '*Chronology ko samjhiye din me Jamia or sham me Shaheen Bagh*' (Understand the chronology, protest at Jamia in the day and Shaheen Bagh in the evening). *The link between Jamia and Shaheen Bagh was integral.*

Women held the microphone at Shaheen Bagh, while men managed the logistics (managing the gate, arranging chairs). One of the most challenging tasks was security since there was such a huge rush. Later, this job became tougher when lumpen elements came and attacked the site.

At the core of the movement were Muslim women, who are often painted as deeply marginalized. The idea of the conservative burqa-clad Muslim woman suggests suppression. This is so in cinema and popular conceptions. The ghoongat and the burqa covering women's heads and faces are at the core of this. The portrayal of Muslim women as separate from other women and Indian society, in general, is pervasive. I recently read an article by Shubhra Gupta on — the movie — *Amar, Akbar, Anthony* (1977). The writer suggested that this film celebrated the idea of secularism.

83

But even in this secularism, the Muslim characters appear as stereotypes. The Hindu character, Amar, played by Vinod Khanna, wears modern clothes and lives in Bombay; while the Christian character, Anthony, played by Amitabh Bachchan, wears a suit and tie and is fluent in English; Akbar, the Muslim character played by Rishi Kapoor, wears a sherwani and topi, speaks Urdu, sings Qawwali, chews pan, and lives in a world of sheltered women. Even in this plural space created by director Manmohan Desai, the Muslim is portrayed in this narrow manner.

Indian Muslim women are not unlike other Indian women, and they are indeed different — in my opinion — from what one reads about Arab Muslim women (although even in the Arab world, there is a wide range in social life). Very few women adopt the burqa, yet it is used to define Muslim women. Most Indian Muslim women appear just like other women, both in dress and ornaments, behaviour, and expectations. Yes, there are hierarchies, but these hierarchies are experienced by all women, even if there are specific ways in which these hierarchies are experienced in different communities.

Shaheen Bagh challenged all the stereotypes and boundaries. It reminded me of Asrarul Haq Majaz:

Tere mathe pe ye anchal bahut hi khuub hai lekin
tu is anchal se ik parcham bana leti to achchha tha
This veil covering your head looks good indeed
but, better, if you'd bear it as a flag.

The *dadis & nanis* (grandmothers) and housewives of Shaheen Bagh sat on the street, defined the protest, took up the charge of Majaz. They were determined to fight the CAA-NRC because it became the symbol of the anti-Muslim politics of the RSS-BJP. They would often finish their housework and then come and sit at the protest site. If they did their cleaning at home, the men did the cleaning at the protest site.

It did not feel that the Muslim community in North India had taken an active role in politics. I thought that we were used as pawns to fulfil others' ambitions. We had become a vote bank for other parties or just data, as Abhay Xaxa said. Even then, the awareness of political trends was minimal, with the situation amongst Muslim women even less clear. Politicisation was near zero. But now, with the rise of the RSS-BJP, new currents emerged since we had lost faith in those so-called secular parties who had taken advantage of us but not done anything for us. Shaheen Bagh is a sign of the shifting trends in northern India.

Women said we would save the Constitution. This is a significant development and shows that the community has become more political by itself. We are not talking about cultural and religious rights, but political rights. We are talking about the rights of a minority in a democratic system. It was not just about CAA-NRC-NPR. It was a protest against stereotypes and created a new standard for Indian politics for women, particularly Muslim women. Shaheen Bagh, which grew out of Jamia, put before the country the view that Muslims want to save the Constitution by demanding that minority rights be enshrined. This was a path for the voiceless. The feeling from Shaheen Bagh spread across northern India and then to the rest of the country. Because of Shaheen Bagh, we saw women — Muslim women — coming onto the streets across India, sitting in the front row and holding public space (such as in Park Circus, Kolkata).

A movement changes not only the society but the individuals who participate in the protest. All those who participated in Shaheen Bagh and the anti-CAA movement have developed a more profound sense of their political identity. The goal was to scrap the CAA. But the more important goal was the creation of tens of thousands of people with political commitment. This developed over the 101 days of Shaheen Bagh. Everyone who joined learned to become a citizen and a leader. I met many students working at the protest site as volunteers, becoming part of the duties and work that each gave the other. There was no explicit leadership, but an organisation was visible to only those who participated. This structure allowed individuals to develop ideas — to set up counters or start painting — and then install them in the encampment space.

The stage became a performance area with speeches, dance, and music — jostling for space and time. Shaheen Bagh became a festival, where people from outside Jamia Nagar who sympathised with the anti-CAA-NRC-NPR movement would come in huge numbers, taking the metro to the Shaheen Bagh metro station and then walking to the site. Students and community members swelled the crowd. Some students started a library at the Shaheen Bagh bus stand; others set up an art gallery for little children. Experienced doctors ran a medical camp; student volunteers from the universities and colleges of Delhi volunteered time there. We had painters and electricians, tea makers and tea servers, and even people who arrived by car and rickshaw with food packets to distribute them in the crowd. Shaheen Bagh is famous for its non-veg food, and many of these eateries were near the encampment; they boomed with business and resistance in this period. The iron footbridge in front of the stage was festooned with posters and pamphlets. The walls were covered with posters, graffiti, and paintings; there was a model of India Gate near the bridge. People were everywhere, raising slogans and singing songs. People did what made them feel comfortable. The atmosphere was that of a political festival in a university. This was a new experience for the people of the area, who had not witnessed anything like this before.

For the local community, the existence of the protest site was a mark of pride. I heard from a friend that he took a rickshaw from Jullena to Shaheen Bagh. When he reached, the rickshawalla refused to take payment. 'Sir', he said, 'I heard that you came from far away to support the cause of Muslims, so I will not take the money'. A friend told me that he saw some people negotiate with an auto-rickshaw driver; when a local guy saw this, he insisted on giving them a ride in his SUV. Others said that restaurant owners gave them a discount when they went to drink tea or eat biryani and nihari.

Some days were extra-special. For instance, there was a rumour that a team from the United Nations (UN) would come to Shaheen Bagh. Large numbers of people came to support the protest site. Even though no UN team arrived, the solidarity was significant. On 26 January 2020, an enormous crowd celebrated the 71st Republic Day at Shaheen Bagh. Three elderly *dadis* of Shaheen Bagh, along with Radhika Vemula (the mother of Rohith Vemula) and Sairo Bano (the mother of the lynching victim Junaid Khan), hoisted the tricolour. The Preamble was read out in English, Hindi, and Urdu. People from all backgrounds came to this place to stand together. We believed in pluralism and humanity. We did not discriminate against anyone. Shaheen Bagh shone with the *idea of India*. We stood that day against discrimination, not just against the CAA.

/   /   /

Everyone had their favourite corner in Shaheen Bagh. I was not attracted to the speeches on the stage. I never attempted to go on stage either. After returning from my hometown, where I attended my brother's wedding, I went to Shaheen Bagh for the first time. This was in January 2020. I had received updates from friends on social media and read the news about this new phenomenon. I wandered through the area, looking at the various manifestations of creativity. There was great energy here, but also, the site had become a tourist hotspot.

On a later visit to Shaheen Bagh, I saw that near the bus stand, there was a blue plastic sheet covering an area. Under that sheet, some people had gathered. I walked there and saw that they'd transformed the bus stand into a library. It was the most fascinating place in the area. As a book lover, I have always fantasised about reading books in different locations. I had this middle-class fantasy to read a book in a park or a café, perhaps on the beach. But I never thought of reading at a bus stand in this way. I was lucky to find this library.

The walls of the library were full of portraits and slogans. There were portraits of Ambedkar, Gandhi, Nehru, Raavan, Fatima Sheikh, and Savitri Phule. Slogans and lyrics of revolutionary songs were on the wall. There was a small bed in one corner, and, on the floor, there were the books. Readers would sit on the floor. A few brick blocks around the bus stand were used as chairs and as a boundary for the library. I'd sit there and hold poetry books in my hand, spending most of my energy observing others and listening to their conversations. This became a kind of hub for discussions. In fact, lectures were held at the library, so that a simple bus stand became a place of profound learning, with various speakers coming to enlighten us about different aspects of our history and our life.

Shaheen Bagh library was not only a cosy place to read. It was filled with philosophy and politics. The name of the library projected a vision. I knew the connection between Fatima Sheikh and Savitri Bai Phule. When Savitri Bai Phule was attacked for promoting education for women in the mid-19th century in Maharashtra, Fatimah Sheikh and her brother Usman Sheikh came to her aid. Only recently have we come to realise the vital role played by Fatima Sheikh in promoting education for women. The library was set up on 17 January and named after both the women. The message was clear: even if education is denied to you, you must be the one to fight for it. The organiser of the library, Mohammed Asif, said, 'These names had been imprinted on their (the protesting women) minds and lips — it is time they imbibe their ideology. Both Fatima Sheikh and Savitribai Phule fought for education in a time when women were systematically kept away from it'.

I believe that one has to be rational enough to consider every form of discrimination, no matter the victim and the perpetrator. We need to condemn any act of discrimination anywhere in the world. This universal attitude toward humanity was evident in

Shaheen Bagh, as it was clear from the library's name. Asif set up the library on 17 January, the death anniversary of Rohit Vemula, a Dalit student at Hyderabad Central University who was a victim of institutional murder. 'This is a symbol of protest', Asif said. 'Rohith's death was institutional murder — the questions he raised; we will continue to reiterate'.

One day, I overheard Asif talking to the media. 'Women and children come out of their houses', he said, 'but the question remains: what are they going to do apart from CAA-NRC-NPR? This is why I came up with the library's idea to educate local people to ask broader questions'. Muslim literacy and education rates are very low. This is especially so in Jamia Nagar. But this library opened some doors. I saw women and men who never read any book come and read at the stand. Many Muslim women get primary education in Urdu and Arabic, especially at home. Asif said he mainly had English books. So those who could read Hindi and Urdu asked for books in their languages but also in English. This was beautiful. People who have never read a single book are ready to read books in a new language, shape a new narrative, and create a new culture.

/   /   /

Jamia students — Kaifi, Kasturi, and others — started *Read for Revolution*, a children's library and gallery. Children would flock there and make about three hundred art pieces each day. These paintings were not just caricatures but serious engagements with the anti-CAA-NRC-NPR protests and issues of discrimination. Kaifi's vision was to engage with the children. 'These children inherit a similar spirit as their mothers do', he said. 'So, it is imperative to engage with their spirit, because people might forget the posters and slogans raised, but children will never forget their knowledge and experience'. The Shaheen Bagh protest, Kaifi said, 'can't be confined to CAA and NRC, because alongside that the historically prevailing gender binary has vehemently been broken down by ordinary women here'.

The students felt that they wanted to restore their library — which had been attacked by the police — at this place. 'If you remove us from our campus, we will use any other public space to start our university', they said. This was also a practical solution. What would the children do as the mothers went to the protest site? Will they sit with their mothers? The idea of the children's library developed as a way to take care of the children while the mothers were at the encampment. The students used a small area in front of two shops that were part of a shopping complex to set up *Read for Revolution*. The book collection at the Fatima Sheikh/Savitri Bai Phule library was for adults. *Read for Revolution* was for small kids, and the space was right near the stage so they could be close to their mothers.

Pictures, pamphlets and paintings adorned the outside of the library. There were two stairs to reach the library. One stairway was closed off by a rope, and only one was in use due to a lack of sufficient volunteers. Volunteers would check to only allow the children in and one or two visitors at a time. Security was a prime issue. The children were young. Their parents had left them there in the trust of the volunteers. The volunteers had to ensure their safety. Only when the parents came to pick them up could the children leave.

Once inside, there were old torn carpets on which the kids sat. In one corner, the organisers used to sit and go through the materials and the papers. There were thousands of children's books. The children flocked to the room in the hundreds, making it impossible to walk around. They would be reading, drawing, and painting. They would do things that they maybe did not have the option to do at home. It was heavenly. The organisers created a small postcard called *Women of Shaheen Bagh*.

/   /   /

Activity filled the space, not only the political programmes but also cultural programmes, which included these libraries. A new language of protest was being created, with songs and poems everywhere. Many artists came to the protest site to contribute with their skills. We saw classical music, rap, contemporary pop songs, theatre, dance, and graffiti. One evening, I was going home from Shaheen Bagh. I knew my favourite singer, Shubha Mudgal, was coming to perform at the site. Due to some urgency, I had to go home. While walking along, I heard her voice. Since the protest site went on for more than a kilometre, the organisers had installed speakers along the road. The performance echoed through the entire area; she sang revolutionary songs, and her voice compelled me to return to the protest site. I attended the whole concert— mesmerized and moved. Her rendition of *Dastoor* by Habib Jalib was beautiful.

Sahmat's Artists Against Communalism organised other singers and performers to come to the site, such as the Carnatic singer T.M. Krishna and songwriter Prateek Kuhad. We had rapper Sumit Roy, poet Aamir Aziz, musicians Ankur Tewari and Saba Azad perform. And we had the Sufi singer Madan Gopal Singh. In 2012, I had heard Madan Gopal Singh with his band *Char Yaar*. After a long wait, I heard him again. Such prominent artists came and performed on our rickety stage rather than in a fancy auditorium. Their dedication and commitment to rationalism and pluralism brought them to Shaheen Bagh.

Women sat in a small shed, where men were not permitted. For a male to reach the stage or go backstage was almost impossible. Speakers and performers could do so, but not others. On the day of Madan Gopal Singh's performance, I somehow managed to go backstage and get a close look at his performance. I felt lucky that I reached there and saw the energy. I was mesmerised by his performance. When he was ready to end, a woman started shouting at him to continue, so he did.

/ / /

Around midnight, while I was sitting and enjoying Madan Gopal Singh's performance, one old Sardarji came onto the stage. He went to the moderator of the protest stage and requested to make an announcement, 'Our people from Punjab are coming in 10 buses. Please let people know, they've been stopped by the police nearby and send some people to fetch them'. A volunteer got him a chair and asked him to rest. Another Sardarji came and said, 'No need to panic. No need to go there. Our people will handle the situation'. The crowd relaxed. We continued to enjoy the performance by Madan Gopal Singh.

A delegation of Sikh farmers had travelled from Panjab to Shaheen Bagh in solidarity; the police detained them on the night of 14 January. We are aware of the generosity of the Sikh community. That night, I went home and learned more about them and their glorious and tragic history.

The following day, 15 January, ten buses of Sikh farmers reached the protest. They received a warm welcome from everyone.

However, I did not comprehend the level of their commitment till I saw hundreds of farmers in yellow and green, mostly older women and men, come in smiling. They came with the message of *Quami Ekta Zindabad* (Communal Harmony Long Live)! The emotionally charged environment ringed with the slogan: *bhai naal bhai nu ladan nee dena, san santali banan ni dena* (May brothers never fight again, may 1947 never be repeated). They understood the pain of Muslims fearing disenfranchisement from CAA & NRC.

With their arrival, the image of Shaheen Bagh became even more beautiful; it became complete. We felt like we were walking in a mustard field, colourful and fertile. Almost all the farmers were elderly. We felt strangely protected and secure. 'Don't worry, we will win the fight', they said. Each person on the stage had said this, but I felt comforted when the Sardars said these words.

One evening, a young Sardar with a yellow turban raised revolutionary slogans. I was amazed to see that. I was confused. The contingent that had come here were mainly elderly Sardars. Where did this young boy come from? Then I saw a friend wearing a turban. I asked him what was going on. 'In Shaheen Bagh', he replied, 'everybody is wearing a turban today'. I walked to the shed and found the Sikh farmers wrapping turbans on the heads of the children. I asked one Sardar why he was wrapping turbans. He told me that people came in with plain cloth and asked them to put turbans on them. Such a beautiful image! Shaheen Bagh looked like Punjab with yellow turbans, a place of peace and love. This was the best moment of the Shaheen Bagh protest.

/   /   /

By 17 December, Jamia had become one of the centres of the protest against CAA-NRC-NPR. I was standing with my friends in a corner when I saw a Nihang Sikh walk towards us. I went to him and greeted him. He greeted me back. Many people gathered around us. I tried to ask him what he was doing. He said he was from Bhatinda, and he had come to Jamia the previous night. 'I go to where people are discriminated', he said, 'so when I got the news of the crackdown, I came here. Though I was supposed to go somewhere else to settle the dispute of a Gurudwara, I choose to come here because there will be other people to save that Gurudwara'. This melted our hearts, and we thanked him for his concern and generosity. I asked him where he was staying. He said he was staying at the Jamia mosque. I was so pleased that a Sikh was staying at a mosque. In this atmosphere of communalism, this is an example of love and peace.

When the Sikh farmers came to Shaheen Bagh, they brought one core aspect of their tradition: to feed people. Till then, individuals and groups brought food in solidarity. Now, the Sikh farmers set up langar and made food there. We now had a community kitchen at the site.

General Secretary of the farmer organisation BKU (Ekta Ugrahan) Sukhdev Singh Kokri said, 'We will take along rations to organise *langar* for protesters till 8 February. We feel it is our ethical duty to stand by our Muslim brothers and sisters'. The langar has a natural power to attract everyone; food connects the entire community and forms a great bridge between people.

My father told me that Sikh people should be welcomed with flowers because of their dedication to justice. 'I don't know from where they get such love and dedication', my father asked. I don't know either. I read somewhere about the teachings of Guru Gobind Singh, which opposed oppression in all forms. I wish everybody would learn this kind of lesson. All these thoughts gathered around as we began to consider that this area was not immune from the massive anti-Sikh violence of 1984. One of my Malayali friends asked a rickshawalla about Jamia Nagar. 'During the 1984 anti-Sikh pogrom', he said, 'those Sikhs who lived here and there, scattered, were massacred, and those who lived together managed to survive'. The lesson of 1984 sent fear through Muslims, who then moved in more significant numbers into Jamia Nagar. They worried that they would be killed in a riot. After the riots of 1992, more Muslims moved into the area. The mixed locality became less and less diverse.

Ek admi ka marna maut hai
Ek lakh admiyo ko marna tamasha
When one person is killed, it's death
When a million die, it's a spectacle
~ Saadat Hasan Manto

There is a connection between the anti-Sikh riots of 1984 and the anti-Muslim riots of 2002. These riots are done by the powerful against the less powerful, primarily Hindus against Sikhs, damaging the fabric of humanity. When someone is murdered in such riots, it is the death of a human, but when everyone is silent, it is the death of humanity. In my hometown, I heard that everyone looted the shops of the Sikhs in 1984, people of all other faiths and all castes. That famous poem by Martin Niemoller comes to mind:

First, they came for the socialists, and I did not speak out —
Because I was not a socialist.
Then they came for the trade unionists, and I did not speak out —
Because I was not a trade unionist.
Then they came for the Jews, and I did not speak out —
Because I was not a Jew.
Then they came for me — and there was no one left to speak for me.

My grandfather was a principled man of solid moral courage. He worked at the Bokaro Steel plant. People of all communities respected him. He told me that in 1984 he saw a mob attacking a Sikh man. My grandfather tried to stop them. One man said, 'We will not leave him because these Sikhs killed our Indiraji. So, we are requesting you to go'. My grandfather said, 'If you are not going to stop, don't toy with him. Kill him in one go so that he does not have to bear this traumatic end'. My grandfather failed to save him. He was alone. One cannot do these things alone. The entire community is necessary. My father told me that on the same day he reached Delhi in 1984 and stepped out of the train, he could not walk on the railway station because hundreds of dead bodies were lying on the platform. When the Sikhs were killed and displaced, their property was seized and sold at low prices. Humanity is reduced to this level. I remember one scene from Khuswant Singh's

Delhi (1990) about a community reduced to being a spectator of terrible violence, thinking only about their luxury:

> I stay rooted to the ground and peer through the bush. I see a fellow reading something from a paper in his hand. He points to a garage owned by Sikh mechanics — the mob moves to the garages. Cars lined outside for repairs are set on fire. Garage doors smashed open. People watch them from their balconies. Someone pleads, 'These cars belong to Hindus; the Sikh mechanics have fled. If you set fire to the garages, the whole building will catch fire. We are only Hindus, Muslims, and Christians here. Why don't you go to the taxi-stand?'

> People stood on their balconies. They told the mob where to go and what to do. They were inflaming the situation. Instead of saving them, they were telling them how to get them. In a nutshell, if you see any discrimination, please come out of our balcony and stop them; if you are unable to do so, at least hold tight to sympathy in your heart instead of supporting the mob. No matter what you are, if you will not come out from your balcony, then nobody will come to you from their balcony for you.

/   /   /

The Delhi Vidhan Sabha election was scheduled for 8 February 2020 amid these protests. The protest at Shaheen Bagh took hold in the election campaigning. The leading contenders were the Bharatiya Janta Party (BJP) and the Aam Aadmi Party (AAP). The BJP focused on Shaheen Bagh. They did not have any development agenda. They painted Shaheen Bagh as a Muslim movement, an anti-national movement and not a movement to save the Constitution. They used Shaheen Bagh to polarise the voters. The slogans were chilling: *Desh ke gaddaro ko, goli maro salo ko* (Shoot the traitors to the nation). This was a call for violence. Election day was compared to an India-Pakistan cricket match, and they spoke of a 'surgical strike' on Shaheen Bagh. This kind of violent talk provoked incidents of firing and hurling of petrol bombs. But it was nothing like what was to unfold in North East Delhi from 23 February.

On 2 February, the Hindu Sena — an extreme-right group — warned that they would come and vacate Shaheen Bagh by force. In an interview with *India Today*, the Hindu Sena chief said, 'Lakhs of people are suffering because of the closure of the Shaheen Bagh road due to the protests. And most importantly, Shaheen Bagh has become a hub of anti-national voices, where time and again, "anti-Hindu" voices and elements that incite people to go against the country and divide the country are cropping up'. The Hindu Sena was encouraged by the police to call off their march. Everyone still anticipated violence. People rushed to the site to defend it. That night I met two people who came to save the protest. One was my professor Kamini Sharma, a 67-year-old woman — she sat at the barricade. Another was Amar Jha, a retired scientist from Dwarka to save Shaheen Bagh. I met Amar Jha at 10 pm as he stood bravely in the chilly winter. He introduced me to his friends and said, 'When I saw the news that someone is coming to attack Shaheen Bagh, I asked my friends to join me to save the protest'. I did not know anything about him. But his sincere energy was marvellous. His dialogue was filmy, with phrases such as, '*ane do hum dekh lenge*' (bring it on, we'll handle them).

On 24 March 2020, the police vacated Shaheen Bagh because of the COVID-19 pandemic; this was after 101 days. Shaheen Bagh did not succeed in the CAA withdrawal or any of the other policies, but it did put the government and the country on notice. It showed that Muslim women were not going to tolerate discrimination and the violation of the Constitution. It showed that very large numbers of people would stand with them.

6. RESISTANCE THROUGH ART

Main kali takhti pe safed chauk istemal karta hu, taki kali
takhti aur numaya ho jaye
On the black slate, I write with white chalk to further showcase
its darkness

~ Saadat Hasan Manto

Art is crucial to revolutionary traditions. This was the case in the October Revolution of 1917, and it is crucial to the left history in India. One of my favourite poets who emerges from these traditions is Makhdoom Mohiuddin (1908–1969). Makhdoom became a household name during the Telangana movement against the Nizam of Hyderabad in 1946–47. He was deeply influenced by Soviet literature, which had come to him through the Communist Party of India, of which he was a member. Due to his membership in the Communist Party, Makhdoom visited the USSR, the communist states in Eastern Europe, and the People's Republic of China. He experienced the great cultural experiment of transforming feudal society into a modern society and making democracy part of the everyday life of people and not just of an electoral process. Makhdoom was known as the *Shayar-e-Inqilab*, the poet of the revolution. He brought together the cultural ethos of Urdu poetry, Communism, Soviet realism, and art traditions of Telugu-speaking peoples. His poetry is easy to understand and transport, and like the poetry of other revolutionary poets, inspires people to his social vision:

Hayat le ke chalo qaenat le ke chalo
chalo to sare zamane ko sath le ke chalo

Bear Life and the World in the same stride
and when you walk, take everyone along.

Makhdoom wrote to inspire the cadre and the ordinary citizen. His poetry spoke for the equal world we want to build. He wrote many poems as part of the Telangana movement. I like this one because it speaks in the feminine, which is uncommon in Urdu revolutionary poetry:

Phirne wali khet ke medo pe bal khati hui,
nazam-o-sheereen qehqaho ke phool barsati hui,
kangano se khelte auro se sharmati hui,
ajnabi ko dekh kar khamosh mat ho, gaye ja
ha telangan gaye ja, bankee telangan gaye ja
O wanderer woman flickering on the weirs of fields
showering flowers with soften and sweeten words
playing with bangles and shying from others
don't be silent while seeing strangers, sing
O Telangan keep singing, Telangan keep singing.

The richness of left political culture has not broadly become part of Indian culture. It is undoubtedly part of our left student culture, and it is a part of the pockets of the left movements across the country. While such rich cultural explosions emerge out of left politics, they are absent in the right, even in mass movements like the JP movement led by Jayaprakash Narayan in the 1970s and the India Against Corruption movement led by Anna Hazare of 2011. They were not capable of producing the kind of rich culture that came from the pen of Makhdoom.

In 2015, I was reading *Mother* by Maxim Gorky while visiting a friend in Calicut, Kerala. During that time, the campaign for the Panchayat elections was in full swing. I saw reflections from the novel, the cultural excitement mirroring what Gorky had described as the factory labour's hard life generating the revolutionary energy of the 1905 Russian Revolution. I saw this kind of cultural energy during both the Jamia protests and at Shaheen Bagh. Anti-CAA protests brought artistic energy out into the open, something unusual in northern India. From graffiti and calligraphy to songs and slogans, the air of Delhi rang with the hope of a different culture.

/   /   /

When I returned from my brother's wedding in January 2020, I craved to feel the energy of the graffiti at Jamia again. I wanted to be part of the electrical political process I'd experienced during the Kerala panchayat elections in 2015, and at Jamia in 2019, I wanted to be a part of hope. In Jamia, the festivities were concentrated at the Maulana Mohammad Ali Jauhar Marg since the university was closed, and students were not permitted to return to the campus.

I parked my bike at the side of the road and walked from the Ansari auditorium to the Holy Family Hospital. One side of the road was barricaded with rope. The other side had temporary stands selling food, books, and posters, including the sale of tricolour flags; there was a library and a tea stall. Students and community people went from counter to counter, sipping tea and chatting. I did not see any familiar faces as I meandered through the crowd. In front of Gate no. 7, there was a stage covered with a massive poster of the Preamble. There were also posters of Babasaheb Bhimrao Ambedkar, Bhagat Singh, Chandrashekhar Azad, Chandrashekhar Azad Ravan, Faiz Ahmed Faiz, Karl Marx, Mahatma Gandhi, Maulana Mohammad Ali Jauhar, and Zakir Husain. I felt my university had matured into a richer *idea of India*, drawing in icons from the freedom movement and beyond.

Slogans and messages from various people and organisations covered the area near the stage. On the stage, there was a speaker on which songs were being played. I left the stage area and went to the Faculty of Engineering, where I saw some students make graffiti on the wall of the university stadium. The stadium has a boundary made of an iron sheet, which is a perfect canvas for graffiti. It already carried some typographical art in English, Hindi, and Urdu. The wall was dedicated to the struggle. People walking by stopped and took photos and selfies; they seemed attracted to the universal messages painted there. In my view, graffiti is an essential component of popular protest and cultural heritage. The strong visuals — vibrant colours, words and images — instantly attract us. Even if people disagree with the protest, they are drawn to the graffiti. A driver for the Gramin Sewa stopped and gave the artists a thumbs up. As people walked by, they stopped to look at the art and talk to the artists; they supported the art wholeheartedly.

I went to the artists to talk to them about the slogans and couplets on the wall. A few students were drawing the border for the graffiti nearby. A petite guy who looked like an artist was standing on an aluminium ladder and writing some letters in a blue pencil. I strained to read the words as I am not a proficient Nastaliq reader. Up-close, I realized the calligraphy was flawless, and I slowly read it out; they were my favourite lines from Faiz:

Jis dhaj se koi maqtal men gaya vo shan salamat rehti hai
ye jan to ani jani hai is jan ki koi bat nahi
The pride with which one walks to the gallows remains
life as such is a feeble thing; it's here now and gone the next, it
doesn't matter

I saw another poem at the gate of the university stadium. It had been sprayed hastily and did not seem as artistic as the previous one. However, the urgency of the spray paint drew me in, and I saw a favourite poem written by Paash (1950–1988):

Main ghas hoon
main apke har kiye-dhare par ug aoonga

bam fenk do chahe vishvavidyalay par
bana do hostel ko malbe ka dher
suhaga phira do bhale hi hamari jhopdiyon par
mera kya karoge
main to ghas hoon har chiz par ug aoonga
Bange ko dher kar do
Sangaroor mita dalo
dhool men mila do Ludhiyana zila
meri hariyali apna kam karegi . . .
do sal . . . das sal bad
savariyan phir kisi conductor se poochhengi
yeh kaun-si jagah hai
mujhe Baranala utar dena
jahan hare ghas ka jangal hai
main ghas hoon, main apana kam karoonga
main apake har kiye-dhare par ug aoonga
I am grass
I will sprout through and cover every deed you commit
you may bomb the universities
reduce the hostels into heaps of rubble
or you may bulldoze over our homes
but you cannot erase me
because I am grass
I will sprout through your every deed
you may:
shoot down Banga
erase Sangrur off the map
crush down Ludhiana into dust
my resilience will do its work . . .
after two years . . . after ten years
my green mantle will cover everything
comrades would again ask some conductor:
what place is this?
Drop me at Barnala

where thick green jungle grows
I am grass; I will do my work
I will sprout out through every deed you may commit

Since the rise of the anti-CAA movement, the *ghas* (grass) by Paash had been used metaphorically by the protestors. It was as if he had written the poem for the 15 December crackdown. When we were at the library that day, the police fired tear gas into the university. There was fear in us, the feeling of being merely grass, to be trampled under feet.

Bam fek do chahe vishvavidyalay par
bana do hostel ko malbe ka dher
main ghas hoon, main apana kam karoonga
main apake har kiye-dhare par ug aoonga
You may bomb the universities
reduce the hostel into heaps of rubble
but you cannot erase me
because I am grass
I will sprout through every deed you commit

I read this numerous times. Then I went along to see the other graffiti. *Hum ladenge sathi* (We shall fight, comrade), a stanza of the Paash poem, beautifully decorated the Jamia canvas. Paash was the poet of the marginal and the poor. He gave us words to express our anti-CAA movement. 'We the people of India are not going to accept this', we seemed to be saying, 'and we will fight back'. Paash's poetry gave us that energy to fight back.

Hum ladenge jab tak
duniya mein ladne ki zarurat baqi hogi
We shall fight
till the need to fight exists

This was a universal message. We will fight injustice committed against any part of humanity.

I recognised one of the artists from the campus with who I'd previously interacted with. Her name was Simeen Anjum, a second-year student of fine arts. I said, 'I did not know anyone, so I was loitering around. I am neither a student leader nor affiliated with any political party. I do not have predefined duties in the protest. I am not sure what I can do; please tell me where should I begin?' She asked me to hold the paint. I felt happy about meeting someone I recognised. I am terrible at creative work but enjoy being creative. I am a terrible singer, but I love songs. I am a terrible poet but love to write poetry. I am awful at painting but have always wanted to paint.

We were motivated and encouraged to contribute what we could towards the anti-CAA movement, which I did when I joined the graffiti artists. I knew that if I tried to paint on the wall, it would not be about passing or failing an exam but about being a small part of a glorious movement. Simeen was one of the leaders of the group — the Graffiti Queen! She brimmed with infectious energy, and her management skills were impressive. Simeen welcomed me to the group and taught me how to hold the brush correctly. I observed her painting murals, eager to help. I could've also been an errand boy to bring supplies and other necessities; all I wanted to do was contribute. She dried her brush in turpentine oil and asked me to hold it, go on the ladder and start painting an entire area. I was unsure what to do. She then patiently explained to me, 'I need a huge red-coloured background for a new graffiti. Making a background is primary and easy, so start here. Later, I will assign you other work'. I was hesitant. 'I'm the worst artist', I said. 'Art comes out of a mistake, and you are free to do as you please; we will fix it', she replied. 'Within this boundary, feel free to create the art you want'. Her words gave me confidence. I started to paint.

One of the professional artists, Mushtaq Bhai, said, '*ap hum sab ko bewaquf bana rahe thei ap kitna achha brush chala rahe hain'* (you've been underplaying your painting skills). Simeen's faith transformed me into an artist. What was extraordinary was that she gave a chance to everyone. Since then, I became a part of the creative team of the anti-CAA-NRC-NPR movement. After Simeen, Mushtaq Bhai was my favourite person in the group. He was an unemployed, professional painter. He'd aspired to join the armed forces as a child, but ill-health kept him from realizing his dreams. He told me that he saw the artists painting a mural one day, while passing by. He spoke to them, moved by their commitment, he instantly decided to join the group. His skills were an asset for us. The graffiti and slogans, which had begun as a spontaneous response to 15 December, were now growing beyond the students and campus.

I went there every morning to work. Gradually, I became an integral part of the team, working on design and execution. We had rigorous brainstorming sessions about the content and funding of our work. Funding was the simpler part; reaching an agreement on what to paint was difficult. Each member of the team participated in these discussions. A senior research scholar who came every evening and other passers-by also contributed their ideas. Our group had two kinds of people: those who were more artistic and those who were more political. Both were necessary. Political ideology and clarity are crucial for the process of graffiti making because graffiti is political art.

The graffiti was not merely for the Jamia students. It was for everybody. Historically, graffiti has been an essential tool to creatively express sociopolitical discontent and, hence, vital to our cultural heritage. That is why the content's language, ideology, sensitivity, and relevance were critical. We aimed to make our art easily accessible to the larger community and decided our best to incorporate Hindustani, Hindi, and Urdu — the common languages of northern India. Our college protest had become part of a community protest — with Jamia and Shaheen Bagh as one — which meant that our visual vocabulary had to evolve beyond the students.

We decided to do our fifth graffiti only in Hindi; a visiting senior research scholar suggested working with Ramdhari Singh Dinkar's poetry. One of our more politically-inclined artists refused the suggestion and said, 'Dinkar was a poet of establishment, and our graffiti should be radical . . . we should have a revolutionary and anti-establishment poet, and not someone who gave moral lessons to the disenfranchised'. I listened silently, unaware of Dinkar's politics and poetry. Simeen watched the situation calmly and suggested that we discuss this later. We went home.

The senior research scholar was present the next day, and the discussion continued. He wanted us to write out a stanza from Dinkar. Simeen didn't want any friction. For her, graffiti was a means to protest, to put forth the anguish and pain of December 15 and onwards; all she wanted was a compelling message to go on the wall. The discussion continued. The lines selected from Dinkar were:

Samar shes hai
nahi pap ka bhagi kewal vyadh jo tatsath hai
samay likhega unka bhi apradh
The war is incomplete yet
not only the murderer is a sinner
history shall also record the sins of those
who merely stood and watched

I disagreed with this idea, and I believed it was unwise to write difficult Sanskritic Hindi. The audience, not only the students but the greater community, even those who cannot read, should comprehend the larger message at a glance; if they are unable to do so, it can be alienating. The senior was adamant. He said, 'If people do not understand, they will Google it; everybody has a smartphone'. Simeen agreed that it was difficult to comprehend. We did not paint it.

I called a poet friend, Ahona, and asked for suggestions from Hindi poetry. She suggested Sarveshwar Dayal Saxena. The lines were:

Bhediye ki ankhein surkh hain, use tab tak ghuro
jab tak tumhari ankhein surkh na ho jayein
The wolf's eyes are bloodthirsty red
keep staring
until your eyes
turn red, too

The discussion was far from over. One of Jamia's well-known artists came over and suggested an image with the poetry. He said we could draw a small girl looking into the eyes of the police, dressed in full riot gear. We began our work. When something significant took place, we introduced new graphics and texts, updating our walls like websites. For instance, on 30 January, when the Jamia students marched, and a person opened fire at them, we illustrated the incident on the wall.

One Sunday, I came to the graffiti spot. There were a hundred artists there; several came on their own, many were painting on the road. I saw some people writing Urdu poetry while others drew cartoons. That day, Jamia was filled with colour. I met an old friend, painting Faiz Ahmed Faiz's famous poem *Hum Dekhenge* on the wall. Most of the artists were politically left-inclined.

In Eduardo Galeano's words: Walls are the publishers of the poor. Protest art in the form of graffiti has always been part of the left's political culture, drawing in images and personalities, poems, and slogans from the left heritage. We had limitations, however. We failed to highlight the Muslim and Dalit questions on the walls.

We drew Akhil Gogoi there and Chandrashekhar Azad Ravan because both were part of the anti-CAA movement; when goons attacked JNUSU president Aishe Ghosh on 5 January 2020, we made a portrait of her on one of the walls; and we even made a visual of the Australian forest fires.

However, we later realised that we did not make graffiti explicitly representing Muslims. A different art group had made a portrait of Malcolm X and a portrait of the missing JNU scholar Najeeb Ahmed. I discussed this with my art group, and they too realised this mistake.

Muslims have been reduced to data and vote banks in the name of *Ganga-Jamuni Tehzeeb*. This was a limitation. As the Adivasi activist Abhay Flavian Xaxa put it, 'I am not your data, nor am I your vote bank'.

An older man came every day and gave us crates of juice. We were hesitant to take it. One day he said, 'I cannot do anything for this county and the movement. I am a salesman who doesn't have time, so please let me contribute this way'. That was a perfect picture of the mood of our movement.

/   /   /

I was part of the graffiti team, but apart from being an errand boy, I was also tasked with explaining the graffiti to visitors. I enjoyed it because I got to interact with people from different backgrounds. My favourite visitors were school students who got off their school buses and saw the murals. They expressed their appreciation for the art with a pure heart.

There were two types of visitors: students and other educated people, and the larger community from Jamia. The reactions of the local community were enlightening. They would like to talk to us about what was drawn on the wall. Some people — like the salesman — would bring juice and water for us as gifts. We were treated with extraordinary amounts of love; the local community began to understand graffiti making. Once exposed to this kind of art, they tried to become a part of it. Graffiti did not only adorn the wall, but it was educational in form and content. They began to suggest that we do this or that drawing. It would often lead to a discussion. I would enjoy this, but to be honest — it would sometimes get very trying. The suggestions, however, showed that people had ample latent feelings and ideas about both politics and art. This was very welcome learning. One day I called my professor, who had lived in Jamia for a decade and talked to her about all this. She said that it is true that these kinds of movements can politicise people and create political energy that draws people to get involved in things. How to channel their energy? They do not have the luxury to write a blog or tweet or have an opinion piece published in the newspaper or on the web. How do we get ordinary people the space to express themselves?

For the next few days, these questions occupied me. With some friends from Jamia, I decided to start a counter called — Write for Revolution. On 20 January 2020, we occupied a space near the pavement near Gate no. 7, decorated it and began our work. Every afternoon, we would gather at Gate no. 7, put a small carpet on the pavement and write; we hung up posters and paintings. We put several pens and note pads on the carpet to enable people to express themselves. To better explain what Write for Revolution was, we deployed four or five volunteers on the road.

Writing is a tedious job. It required effort to convince people to join. Those who did were happy with their experience. When people finished writing about the CAA-NRC, they would ask, 'are you going to publish it?'. We would tell them that we collected all the texts and later upload them onto social media sites. At a later stage, we might compile a book. We would write till 7 pm, then go to a friend's house to discuss our daily output and read the writings. We published the best writings on social media. After some time, we made a counter at Shaheen Bagh, near the Fatima Sheikh–Savitri Bai Phule library. When the energy at Jamia shifted to Shaheen Bagh, we would mostly work there. We wrote the following on social media:

Write for Revolution is a platform created by the students of Jamia to protest against CAA, NPR and NRC. Come and express your views by writing down your views or by depicting them through art of any kind. Write for Revolution provides you the platforms to send your message to the authority. This is the most civilised way of expressing views. With this platform you can express your feeling, emotions and tell the authorities what you need.

Our primary focus was to engage with the community only because their writings were raw and heartfelt. We received lovely write-ups from all parts of society, students and the locals, with a range of political experience. A young girl named Kavita wrote the most heartfelt message, which asked a question of authority:

My boyfriend is Muslim if he will go to detention, will I be able to go with him because I am Hindu?

A student from Amity University, Phyba, wrote this compelling message:

The real minority of India is the Indians, rest of the people are just busy calling themselves Hindus and Muslims.

The Hindi poet, Vijay Singh Thakur wrote:

Ke likh dil me inqilab kuchh is tarah,
lahu ka har ek qatra sarfarosh ho jaye

A veteran journalist wrote:

Sorry for the traffic troubles, but this is a revolution.

I am more academic than I am an activist. I always look at things from a theoretical point of view. I wanted to bring some of my interests to the protest site. I helped to organise a lecture series from 13 February, and we would go on to hold lectures every second day. The idea came from one of our professors who said, 'Our university has witnessed a crackdown by police and then been locked up. So, as students, we will have to pursue our education outside the classroom. And we will not stop our learning process and learn everything we thought of and not a particular subject or topic'. We wanted to create a *University on the Road*. This would be part of Write for Revolution. Our lecture series was called *Street Lecture Series*. We had conducted four lectures:

1. Dr Rana Safvi, historian, '*Dilli Jo Ek Sheher Tha*' (Delhi, which was once a city.)
2. Gauhar Raza, poet and scientist, 'Love, Poetry, and Resistance'.
3. Dr Amit Ranjan, literary scholar, 'Dara Shikoh: The Price of a Dream'.
4. Dr Rizwan Qaiser, historian, 'Indian Muslims in Historical and Contemporary Perspective'.

Our fifth lecture was to be given by Dr Irfanullah Farooqui on 24 February 2020 on the topic, 'Call Me Not a Poet: Engaging with Iqbal on Iqbal'. But the lecture had to be cancelled because of the pogrom in North East Delhi. That night, during the violence in Delhi, my contribution to the protest ended.

/   /   /

I was not an active participant in the protest and mainly was part of the crowd. I joined the graffiti group only after regularly visiting the site. It felt good to be part of the creative team, and I limited myself to painting the background with the roller. I enjoyed the work, and I liked how it drew people in.

I rarely went near the stage or in front of the audience. Whenever I arrived at Jamia, I went to the graffiti area and then home. When Simeen's team finished the work at Jamia, they moved on to another protest site. Due to the lack of students and their resources, protest art could not flourish in other places. Student volunteers put up many cultural sites with — libraries, art galleries, and graffiti. When my graffiti team left Jamia, I had nothing to do much to do. I began to loiter around again. I had gone back to studying by the time the university reopened. One evening, when I walked by the stage, I saw some of my friends sitting on the road, singing. When I spoke to them, they told me about their group. They used to come to Jamia at 4 pm each day as most of them worked day jobs. They would sit behind the stage and sing for an hour or two and then go to Shaheen Bagh to perform. I realised I had a hidden talent — singing well even if I sometimes struggled to find the apt note. Once on a train to Hyderabad, I played the *antakshari*, and my friends told me that I had a good voice. I believed them and joined these friends.

I am very fond of poetry in various languages. I read and listen to poetry in different languages without even understanding a word. I love the rendition of poetry — the singing and the reciting — as much as the reading of poetry. I fell in love with poetry because I loved Jagjit Singh, Ghulam Ali, and Mehdi Hasan's renditions, and in all likelihood, I cultivated this appreciation from my father. Thus, it is one of the reasons that I felt like singing the very moment I joined that group. The group comprised six or seven people, sitting in a circle and singing with about fifty people in the audience who joined the chorus. The six or seven sang revolutionary songs, the lyrics on their mobile phones; they sang

Dushyant Kumar, Faiz Ahmed Faiz, Habib Jalib, and others. The singers were not from any theatre or singing group, yet they sang perfectly. They sang these three poems continuously:

Ho Gayi Hai Pir Parvat
~ Dushyant Kumar

Ho gayi hai pir parvat-si pighalani chahiye
is Himalay se koi Ganga nikalani chahiye
aj yah divar, paradon ki tarah hilane lagi
shart thi lekin ki ye buniyad hilani chahiye
har sadk par, har gali men, har nagar, har ganv men
hath laharate hue har lash chalani chahiye
sirf hangama khada karana mera maqsad nahin
meri koshish hai ki ye soorat badalni chahiye
mere seene men nahin to tere seene men sahi
ho kahin bhi aag, lekin aag jalni chahiye

This Pain Has Frozen Into a Mountain

This pain has frozen into a mountain; it shall melt
a river shall gush out from this Himalaya
Today as a curtain, this wall quivers
but, we promised to shake its very foundations
In every town, in every village, on every street, in every lane
every corpse shall walk waving hands
It is not my intention to merely raise a hollow uproar
I insist the present situation be changed
If not in mine, then in your bosom
wherever is the spark it shall ignite fire

/   /   /

Hum Dekhenge
~ Faiz Ahmed Faiz

Hum dekhenge
lazim hai ki hum bhi dekhenge
vo din ki jisaka vada hai
jo loh-e-azal men likha hai
jab zulm-o-sitam ke koh-e-garan
rui ki tarah ud jayenge
ham mahaqumon ke panv tale
ye dharati dhad-dhad dhadkegi
aur ahal-e-haqam ke sar oopar
jab bijali kad-kad kadkegi
jab arz-e-khuda ke kabe se
sab but uthavae jayenge
hum ahal-e-safa, maradood-e-haram
masanad pe bithaye jayenge
sab taj uchhale jayenge
sab takht giraye jayenge
bas nam rahega allah ka
jo gayab bhi hai hazir bhi
jo manzar bhi hai nazir bhi
utthega an-al-haq ka nara
jo main bhi hoon aur tum bhi ho
aur raj karegi khulk-e-khuda
jo main bhi hoon aur tum bhi ho

We Shall See

We shall see
we indeed shall also see the day
the promised day
recorded in the book of eternity/justice
when mountains of tyranny and oppression

would blow away like flakes of cotton
when the earth would trample
beneath the feet of the oppressed
when crackling thunders would rage
over the head of the oppressors
when all the idols would be lifted off
from the sacred place
we plebeians, we the banished ones
will be made to sit on the thrones
all the crowns will be flung away
all the thrones will be pulled down
only his name will remain
the one who is unseen and also ever-present
the one who is the spectacle, the one who is also the viewer
the call of I-am-the-Truth will be raised —
that I am, and that you are too
and the children of God will rule
that I am, and that you are too.

/   /   /

Dastoor
~ Habib Jalib

Deep jisaka mahalat hi mein jale
chand logon ki khushiyon ko lekar chale
vo jo saye mein har masalahat ke pale
aise dastoor ko subh-e benoor ko
main nahin manata, main nahin manata
main bhi khayaf nahin takht-e-dar se
main bhi mansoor hoon kah do agiyar se
kyoon darate ho zindan ki divar se
zulm ki bat ko, jehal ki rat ko
main nahin manata, main nahin manata

phool shakhon pe khilne lage, tum kaho
jam rindon ko milne lage, tum kaho
chak seenon ke silne lage, tum kaho
is khule jhooth ko zehan ki loot ko
main nahin manata, main nahin manata
tumne loota hai sadiyon hamara suqoon
ab na hum par chalega tumhara fusoon
charagar main tumhen kis tarah se kahoon
tum nahin charagar, koi mane magar
main nahin manata, main nahin manata

Frozen Tradition

Whose lamp only lights up the palaces,
cares for the happiness of the few
and lives off the weak
such a hollow tradition, a morning-devoid-of-sunlight
I do not accept; I will not accept.
I am not afraid of the gallows
tell them; I am Mansur — the martyr
then why do you scare me with the iron bars of the prison?
Such oppression, such a prolonged night of ignorance
I do not accept; I will not accept.
Flowers are filling up the branches, you say so.
Poor are being served cups of wine, you say so.
Wounds are now beginning to heal, you say so.
Such white lies, such betrayal of facts
I do not accept; I will not accept.
For centuries you have robbed us of our peace of mind
now your sorcery won't work on us
Why do you pretend to be our messiah?
You aren't any messiah, no matter if anyone accepts you as
one.
I do not accept; I will not accept.

/   /   /

A strong literary flair governed the movement, and my favourite poetry filled the winter air. Poems were brought out from the books and spread like fertile soil. My heart hummed with these poems. Soon I started to sing with the group, and they invited me to Shaheen Bagh to perform. I was thrilled. We practised for two hours and then performed for two hours at Shaheen Bagh; this became our daily routine. Others joined in, and our team grew.

Theatre people joined us, and new songs were introduced to our list: *Kahab ta lag jai dhak se* and *Tu zinda hai, tu zindagi ki jeet par yaqeen kar.* I introduced *Ye galio ke awara kutte* and *Bol ke lab azad hain tere* by Faiz Ahmed Faiz; *Hum ladenge sathi* by Paash; and *Aiye mere adarshwadi man* by Muktibodh. I sang *Hum dekhnege, Dastoor*, and *Ho gayi hai pir parvat* at least thirty times a day, perfecting the lyrics and rendition.

At the Bhajan Mandali, we received requests from the audience to sing those three poems. Interestingly, these three poems were not only my favourite but had also come to define the protest. I noticed everybody had begun to memorise these poems, and they sang with us in a chorus. They knew the lyrics, music, and variations. They felt very comfortable singing, and the same rhythm bound us all.

One of the unique features of the protest was that people from all corners wanted to participate in the protest. They contributed according to their capabilities and interests. Many people liked to sit in front of the stage and hear the speakers, and few wanted to be part of the art gallery, those interested in reading went to the library, while others loitered around. People interested in music and songs came to the rear of the stage; whenever we sat on the ground to sing, people surrounded us — some joined us in the singing, some made videos, and others interacted as an audience. One of the spectators stopped us while we were singing *Hum Dekhenge* and asked us to sing one line and take a pause so they all could follow. It reflected the high level of engagement; the community didn't want to be mere spectators — they wanted to be active participants.

There were several counters for free distribution of food, tea, and water, organised by the people. Everybody was not a speaker or a leader, but they were part of the whole. Around a dozen people served tea, and many people walked with the food items to offer the protestors.

/   /   /

Our songs were poems, the poems of resistance that came from the pens for the oppressed.

As with other movements in India, poetry and other art forms became essential in the anti-CAA movement. Art played a pivotal role to bring in non-political people to bring politics into their lives. The old poets resurfaced: Avtar Singh Sandhu (Paash), Dushyant Kumar, Faiz Ahmed Faiz, Muktibodh, and Sarveshwar Dayal Saxena. And new poets were born: Aamir Aziz, Arivu, Nabiya Khan, Puneet Sharma, Rahat Indori, Sabika Abbas Naqvi, Shivangi Pandey, and Varun Grover.

Faiz wrote *Hum Dekhenge* in 1979, two years after the military coup of General Zia ul Haq; his poems of resistance were banned in Pakistan. In 2020 India, the iconic *Hum Dekhenge* was revived, quoted widely in speeches, songs, postcards, pamphlets, everyday conversation, and even on an armada of paper boats in the heart of Shaheen Bagh. It also created unrest in India and was labelled anti-Hindu after IIT Kanpur students recited the poem in solidarity with the Jamia student. A faculty member complained to the administration by calling the recitation anti-Hindu anti-national. A committee was created to investigate the matter. The expert panel focused on these lines of the poem:

Jab arz-e-khuda ke kabe se
sab but uthwaye jayenge
hum ahl-e-safa mardood-e-haram
masnad par baithaye jayenge

Former Supreme Court judge Markandey Katju translated these lines in the following way:

When from the abode of God (Kaba),
all idols will be removed
then we the faithful, who were debarred from sacred places
will be placed on the royal seat

Katju analysed these lines and then wrote, 'It is alleged that these lines are anti-Hindu as Hindus worship idols, and these lines are clearly against idol worship. But this is only a superficial understanding. Faiz was a lifelong communist, and he could hardly have meant that he wanted the Islamization of society. In fact, it was his antagonist General Zia who wanted this'.

Faiz's poem from Pakistan (1979) to India (2020) captured the oppressor's anxieties and the confidence of the oppressed. People might forget the exact events that led to something, but the poem that emerges from that something and that pain remains eternal; it's alive waiting to be reintegrated into the world through other events. In the film *The Postman*, a character says, 'Poetry doesn't belong to those who write it; it belongs to those who need it'. Rahat Indori's famous line — *Hindustan kisi ke bap ka thodi hai* (Hindustan is no one's property) — can move from the anti-CAA protest to a protest against communal violence to a farmers' protest. Such poems — including Varun Grover's *Kagaz nahi dikhayenege* (We will not show the papers) and Puneet Sharma's *Tum kaun ho bey* (Who the hell are you!) — have the same character. These poems became tools against government repression. Aamir Aziz, a young Muslim, a Jamia alumnus, wrote the poem that best captured the moment.

Here's an extract:

Sab Yad Rakha Jayega

Tum jo mangte ho mujhse mere hone ke kagzat,
apni hasti ka tumko saboot zarur diya jayega,
yeh jung tumhari akhri sans tak karha jayega,
sab yad rakha jayega,
ye bhi yad rakha jayega kis-kis tarah se,
tumne watan ko todne ki sazishein ki,
ye bhi yad rakha jayega kis-kis yatan se,
humne watan ko jodne ki khwahishein ki

Everything Will Be Remembered

You who ask for papers to prove my citizenship
you will be shown evidence of my existence.
This war will/shall be fought till your last breath
and everything would be remembered.
We shall also remember in how many ways you plotted to
break the country
and it shall also be remembered by what all means we tried to
keep the country united.

/   /   /

And then, there was this gem from Varun Grover:

Hum Kagaz Nahi Dikhayenge

Hum kagaz nahi dikhayenge
hum kagaz nahi dikhayenge,
tana-shah ake jayenge,
hum kagaz nahi dikhayenge,

tum ansu gas uchhaloge,
tum zehar ki chai ubaloge,
hum pyar ki shakkar gholke isko,
gatt, gatt, gatt pee jayenge,
hum kagaz nahi dikhayenge.
Ye desh hi apna hasil hai,
jahan ram prasad bhi bismil hai,
mitti ko kaise bantoge,
sabka hi khoon toh shamil hai,
tum police se latth pada doge,
tum metro band kara doge,
hum paidal-paidal ayenge,
hum kagaz nahin dikhayenge.
Hum manji yahin bichhayenge,
hum kagaz nahin dikhayenge,
hum sanwidhan ko bachayenge,
hum kagaz nahin dikhayenge,
hum Jan-Gan-Man bhi gayenge,
hum kagaz nahin dikhayenge,
tum jat-pat se bantoge,
hum bhat mangte jayenge,
hum kagaz nahin dikhayenge,
hum kagaz nahin dikhayenge.

We Won't Show the Papers

We won't show the papers
dictators may come and go
we won't show the papers
you may throw tear-gas bombs
you may brew poison in our tea
adding love to it
slurp, slurp, we shall drink it all
but we won't show the papers.

This nation is all we have
where Ram Prasad is also Bismil
everybody's blood and sweat has made this land,
how will you separate it then?
You may get us beaten by police
you may stop the trains
we will come walking on foot
we won't show the papers
we will pitch our tents here
we won't show the papers
we will protect the Constitution
we will sing Jan Gan Man
you may divide us into caste and religion
we will keep asking for bread
but we won't show the papers.

There is a difference between Varun Grover's *Kagaz nahi dikhayenge* (We will not show the papers) and Aamir Aziz's *Sab kuch yad rakha jayega* (Everything will be remembered). Aamir Aziz expressed his pain, the helplessness that made him write this brilliant poem, and that pain and helplessness gives intensity to his words and images. It matters how one's identity is located. Pink Floyd's Roger Waters picked Aamir Aziz's poem and read it out at a protest in London. It moved him.

On his Facebook account, Puneet Sharma published his poem — *Tum kaun ho bey* (Who the hell are you!). His poem is an account of an individual and their unique relationship with their country. Nobody can dictate how one should love their country. That's how Puneet Sharma summed up the poem.

Another poet and Jamia student, Shivangi, a friend, wrote this poem about helplessness. She is not as well-known as the others, but the political chaos impacted her relationship with her Muslim partner.

Mile bhi ho to us kharabe mein
jahan tumhare aur mere bad
shayad cheelon ko hamari haddiya nasib na hon
mile bhi ho to ab mile ho
jab bahar ka bas khayal bhar
meri aur tumhari yadon me baqi hai
mile bhi ho to ab
jab main andar se khali hun
jab mujhme se sab kuch
beh gaya hai
sadak par bahte khoon ke sath.
Ab milne ka kya matlb hai
jab hamare milne ko bag nahi hain,
jab nadiyo ke kinaron par
lasho ki badbu hai,
jab jeth ki dhoop me
tum, main, hamara sab kuchh
jal raha hai,
hamare sab log jal gaye hain
ab milne ka kya matlb hai . . .

You have met me now, in this ruckus
when after we are gone
even vultures may not find our bones to gnaw at.
You met me, but it is now you have met me
when the season of spring
merely exists in our distant memories
you have met me now
when I am hollowed from within,
when everything has flown away
with running blood on the streets
What may come of such a meeting?
when no orchids/gardens entice
when banks of the river are strewn with stinking corpses

when you, me and everything belonging to us
is melting away under the sun
all our people have burnt to ashes
what may come of such a meeting . . .

/   /   /

On 14 January 2020, a rap song written and sung by a Tamil rapper, lyricist, and singer Arivarasu Kalainesan, famously known as Arivu, released a piece on the anti-CAA-NRC movement titled *Sanda Seivom*. His poetic imagination defines this movement from a different standpoint. The song begins with the Ambedkar and Periyar, and he describes the minority and majority politics from a Marxist perspective and stating:

'Who is a minority here? Working-class is the majority around the world'.

In his Youtube description, Arivu defines this song as:

Sanda Seivom
In solidarity with the CAA protests happening all over the country and to the students who are sacrificing their valuable time and energy for a SECULAR SOCIETY and to SAVE THE CONSTITUTION OF INDIA.
"We are Indians, firstly and lastly." ~ Dr B. R. Ambedkar

He performed this song in solidarity with the anti-CAA protest. However, this song did not gain popularity in North India, probably because of the language barrier and Hindi 'supremacy'.

Let us fight
come forward Tamizha
let us fight
in the streets
let us fight

125

united as one
let us fight
if our rights are taken away
let us fight.

They call me Arivu
I'm one in your family
equality is my dream
Ambedkar and Periyar live forever live on forever
and my rap is the product of their rationality!

Democracy is the face of a free nation
true religion should respect all
law is law only if it supports equality.

The foundation of our constitution is against religious
discrimination
killing secularism a foolish act
so, it's important, to tell the truth.

It's the birthplace of thirukkural and the land of peace
we lived here as so many tribes
then, some people came here on their horses
they subjugated us from then till now
they grabbed our lands, exploited our resources.

Generation after generation, they refused to touch us
they segregated us into separate religions and castes
they getting rich by exploiting our work is what's history.
We cannot forget that,
who is a minority here?
The working class is the majority around the world
but, the reality is that we stay divided!

Those who came after us is after our lives,
while those who are struggling for us are getting shot.
Who should live here?
Who is a citizen?
Who is Indian?
Who is Tamizhan?
Who are you to tell me what I am?
One's motherland is not in their birth.

Hey, kamachi and meenachi,
could you ask what the matter is?
Our motherland is in great crisis
who am I?
Who are you?
Who is your grandfather?
NRC coming to dig all that
Aadhar and voter ID are all useless
now you have to dig out your great,
great grandfather from their grave
do you have brains? You, halfwit
is there any logic in your law?
Do you even have it? do I have it?
Is there any religion to the baby that is yet to be born?
Citizenship is our fundamental right,
to deprive us of that is a great tragedy
feeding fanaticism in the name of religion or language
is none other than a foolish act.

All Indians are not Hindus
and Muslims are not the enemies of Hindus
there is no such a thing as an alien immigrant
this is our earth!
CAA is here to divide us

our people will come forward to question it
do not forget that, it will threaten us very soon
do not subscribe to religious divisions.

All of us are immigrants on the earth
whoever is inciting this war is a businessman!

7. GODI MEDIA

Raja bola raat hai
rani boli raat hai
mantri bola raat hai
santri bola raat hai
yeh subah-subah ki baat hai
The king said it is night
the Queen said it is night
the minister said it is night
the guard said it is night
and this happened just after the dawn.

~ Gorakh Pandey

When I was younger, I heard everyone say that politics must not draw me in. They would say, '*arre beta vo ganda field hai, vo sharifon ki jagah nahin hai*' (Politics is a dirty game, it's not for the respectable). We also heard similar statements about the media.

Media as a profession no longer commands the respect that it once did. Neutrality is no longer in evidence, with tycoons owning media houses linked to political parties and the government. With good reason, we now speak of the *godi media* since the media sits in the laps of the powerful.

On 12 December 2019, the media began to focus on Jamia because of the girls' hostel protest against the CAA. The media concentrated on it for two reasons: the photograph of four girls standing on the wall and addressing the protestors went viral, and only women organised it. It was a powerful visual because it showed women — particularly young Muslim women — at the centre of resistance. The next day, during the protest march, Delhi police did not permit it to proceed beyond the University limits. There was a clash with the police, and we were confused about what was going on. Social media was flooded with images and videos of the attack. The media covered the event as a law and order situation. It appeared as if the police were fighting against a foreign country rather than dealing with university students. The pictures of tear gas and beatings shocked many people.

Social media played a crucial role in the Jamia and Shaheen Bagh movements. Notably, the buzz created by raw footage compelled corporate media to follow suit and report the events. Apart from that, they reported because police violence of this scale in the heart of Delhi, was absolutely shocking! Though some reported only to solidify and promote the narrative of the establishment. It was social media and not legacy media, which exposed this violence. It is easy to be critical of social media but essential to recognise its role in citizen journalism, which was the case during the events of 13–15 December at Jamia. Even before Jamia, we saw the role of social media in Assam, where citizen journalism prodded the corporate media to cover the story before we saw it even in Jamia. But the corporate media gives its spin, more 'Assam is burning' and less 'These are the problems with the CAA'. Anti-CAA protests in Assam had a red-hot intensity, but they were not reported with that same sensation because the region is far from Delhi and is often neglected. Still, the visual images broke through the barriers.

The power of visuals cannot be denied. It meant that the events at Jamia remained in the public consciousness long after they were over. Students who were sent home continued to share the videos. We became visible on the world map. Filmmaker Anurag Kashyap said, 'I came back on Twitter when I saw such horrific scenes of the library'.

The media took a communal view of the events of the anti-CAA protest. They saw it as a Muslim protest; yes, it was a protest led by

Muslims, but it was not — as the media suggested — anti-national or limited to only Muslims. Early into the struggle, I met a man in Shaheen Bagh carrying a Bible. I asked him why he was doing so. 'I wanted to show that I am a Christian and that even I support this movement because anti-CAA is not just about a bill for a particular community. It is to save the Constitution'. When people saw the media, they were angry for this reason. They disliked being portrayed in a communal light. At times, media persons were chased away from Jamia and Shaheen Bagh. Sometimes we had to protect the media, even if we agreed that they were reporting the story in a very biased way — in a godi media way. They refused to see the issue as saving the Constitution and refused to see how women were in the leadership in their own right. Everything was reduced to communal politics, which entirely misses the essence our protest.

8. POGROM

Log toot jate hain ek ghar banane mein
tum taras nahin khate bastiyan jalane mein
People spent years in putting a home together
yet some don't even hesitate in burning them down

~ Bashir Badr

On 24 February 2020, we had scheduled the fifth of our Street Lecture Series with Dr Irfanullah Farooqui. The lecture was to be held at 7 pm. But that day, I noticed that the atmosphere was sad and only a few people came. At that point, I was not aware of what had begun in North East Delhi. Some people came to me and said, let us cancel the lecture. There is a *pogrom* going on. People are being killed. I did not listen to them because I did not understand the intensity of the situation. Dr Farooqui arrived and said, 'I am ready to deliver the lecture, but it is better to cancel it because people are dying in the same city and what is the use of giving an academic lecture'. We cancelled the lecture.

My grandfathers — my *Dada* and my *Dadu* — encouraged my political growth, the former with Urdu newspapers and the latter with BBC News. Later, my elder brother exposed me to English newspapers. At university, my gurus helped me develop critical thinking. This cycle of learning has not stopped. I now learn from my supervisor and friends, who teach me to be a good human being and a citizen.

That was the moment when I lost hope as a citizen of this country. I went into denial. That night, for the first time, I felt like an Indian Muslim or an Indian minority. I felt traumatised in my *own* nation. I live about 15 km away from Jamia. Going home that night felt terrible, the streets deserted. I decided to stop and stay at my friend's house. I decided to travel home in the day. I felt restless. I couldn't talk to anyone, not even my closest friends. That night I was not able to sleep at all. The sound of cars going by felt like the noise of a mob entering our complex. That night I understood the meaning of the word *trauma*. I began to think about how I would save myself and my family from the mob. All the images from North East Delhi kept on running through my mind. I thought, if this continues, then I will surely go mad. I counted the minutes for the sun to rise. I decided to move to the university area because it was too difficult to live so far away and in such an isolated fashion. I did not want to worry my parents, who were already traumatised. So, I told them that I would move closer to the campus because I wanted to access the library late at night. My father agreed, and the following day I took my bedding and a few clothes and moved into a rented place.

I had no link with North East Delhi. I had never been there. Yet, the violence traumatised me. I switched off all social media networks and refused to watch TV. I didn't want to see people being killed, shops and houses burning. After moving to Jamia Nagar, I distanced myself from the protest and decided to focus on my studies. I went to the department library. I read. I escaped. Students began to collect relief materials for the riot victims. They collected goods during the day and transported them to North East Delhi in the evening. I found it unbearable and decided to leave the city for a break. When I returned, the pandemic hit us, and we were in lockdown. The trauma continued. Jamia and JNU students were arrested and struck with the Unlawful Activities (Prevention) Act. I was not active in these protests, just one in the crowd, but it affected me deeply. A friend said, 'you are neither a leader nor associated with any party, and you are not on centre stage also'. Her words relieved me, but my trauma haunted me. I would not pick up the phone if it were from an unknown number. I was part of the protest. It is my democratic right. I am a law-abiding citizen. Why am I so scared?

Pogrom

I heard Amrita Pritam ring in my ears . . .

Aaj ankhan Waris Shah nu kiton qabron vichon bol
te aj kitab-e-ishq da koi agla varka phol
ik roi si dhee Punjab dee tu likh likh mare vain
aj lakkhan dheeyan rondian tainun Warish Shah nu kahan

I summon Waris Shah today
speak from your grave
and add a new page to your book of verse
once a daughter of Panjab wept, you wrote an epic
today numerous daughters weep; why are you quiet?

DECLARATION

Some names have been changed to protect identity.

Poetry is translated by Abhishek Pundir.

The cover image is clicked by Sreekanth Sivadasan and is reproduced with his permission.

The book's title is inspired by Aamir Aziz's poem *Sab yad rakha jayega.*

Most of the poetry included in this book was either written or quoted during the protests against the Citizenship (Amendment) Act; I see this poetry as the poetry of struggle.

The text also contains press releases from the Jamia Coordination Committee, social media posts, and the description of a YouTube video. They've been reproduced verbatim and corrected only for spelling errors.